SECOND CHANCE

SECOND CHANCE

How Career Changers Can Find a Great Job

Mary E. Ghilani

 PRAEGER

AN IMPRINT OF ABC-CLIO, LLC
Santa Barbara, California • Denver, Colorado • Oxford, England

Copyright 2010 by Mary E. Ghilani

All rights reserved. No part of this publication may be reproduced,
stored in a retrieval system, or transmitted, in any form or by any
means, electronic, mechanical, photocopying, recording, or otherwise,
except for the inclusion of brief quotations in a review, without prior
permission in writing from the publisher.

Library of Congress Cataloging-in-Publication Data
Ghilani, Mary E., 1958–
   Second chance : how career changers can find a great job / Mary E. Ghilani.
     p. cm.
   Includes bibliographical references and index.
   ISBN 978-1-59884-358-3 (hard copy : alk. paper) — ISBN 978-1-59884-359-0 (ebook)
  1. Career changes. 2. Job hunting. I. Title.
   HF5384.G485 2010
   650.14—dc22   2010001096

ISBN: 978-1-59884-358-3
EISBN: 978-1-59884-359-0

14 13 12 11 10   1 2 3 4 5

This book is also available on the World Wide Web as an eBook.
Visit www.abc-clio.com for details.

Praeger
An Imprint of ABC-CLIO, LLC

ABC-CLIO, LLC
130 Cremona Drive, P.O. Box 1911
Santa Barbara, California 93116-1911

This book is printed on acid-free paper (∞)

Manufactured in the United States of America

Contents

Acknowledgments   vii

Introduction   ix

  1. Midlife and Retirement Redefined   1

  2. So You Want to Change Your Career   9

  3. Find the Right Job Fit   21

  4. Tell Me About Yourself   25

  5. The Benefits of Your Age and Experience   35

  6. Understand Who You Are   41

  7. Career Change Options   51

  8. Careers to Consider   59

  9. Make a Plan *Before* You Quit Your Job   71

10. Go Back to School   81

11. Update Your Resume and Cover Letter   91

12. Are You Ready to Begin Your Career Change?   101

13. Where to Find Job Openings   107

14. How to Utilize the Latest Technology   113

15. Decode Job Descriptions   119

16. How to Create and Use a Portfolio   125

17. Prepare for the Interview   129

18. Interview with Confidence   137

19. What Employers Really Want   145

20. The Subject of Salary 151

21. After the Interview 155

22. How to Find a Job in a Tight Economy 159

23. The Next Phase of Your Life 163

Appendix: Resume Examples for Career Changers 167

Notes 175

Index 181

ACKNOWLEDGMENTS

This book would not have been written without the students who shared their career stories with me over the years. Their names and identifying features have been changed to retain confidentiality.

I am grateful to Susan Hosage for her insights from a Human Resources point of view. Special thanks to my husband, Chuck, for his continued support and encouragement in my writing career. Thanks also to my editor, Jeff Olson, and the staff at ABC-CLIO.

INTRODUCTION

If you have you ever said to yourself, "I'd rather be doing *anything* else than be at this job!" or "I always wanted to become a _____ [fill in the blank]" or "I wish I'd gone to school when I was in my twenties," then you are probably ready to make a career change. If you are between the ages of 30 and 60 and are searching for a different line of work or a more meaningful way to earn a living, then you have opened the right book!

Whether you are contemplating a career change by choice or by necessity, there is no time like the present to begin the process. Many people hate the thought of changing careers because in their minds it means "starting all over again." But there are no wasted life experiences! Career changers are simply adding another layer of knowledge onto an already solid foundation of work and educational experience. Whether you are 30 or 60, you can use the lessons and experience from the first half of your life to help you create a more satisfying career during the next phase of your working life.

Just as the definition of "retirement" or "middle-age" has changed as a result of the improved health, vitality, and life span of Baby Boomers, so has the meaning of work. On average, today's workers will work for 45 years, change jobs seven or more times, and change career fields three or four times.[1] Given the multidirectional pattern of modern career paths, today's career changers will need to redefine their perceptions of employment, employers, and the meaning of work in general.

Take a moment and think about what you *really* want to do for the rest of your life. Some of you may have thought that you'd never have to ask yourself that question again! Do you want to work part-time or full-time? Is pursuing a long-lost hobby the answer? Are you ready to own your own business, become a consultant, or go back to school to train for a new career? What should you do if you are forced into making an unplanned career change because of unemployment? This book will look at all the options available to midlife career changers, provide self-reflective exercises designed to get you thinking "outside of the box," and help you move beyond your "shoulds."

This book will also provide information about second-career options, future employment trends, and the issues pertinent to the people in midlife.

Chapters 2, 3, and 4 will help you identify the underlying reasons motivating your career change, find the work environment that best fits your work style, and help you identify your skills to answer the most common interviewing question of all: "So, tell me about yourself." Chapter 5 will teach you how to identify, repackage, and sell the value of your age and accumulated work experience to an employer. Chapters 7–10 will discuss career change options, retooling for the future, and how to decrease the risk involved in making a career change.

Chapters 11–21 are devoted to helping career changers successfully navigate the job market. You'll learn how to tailor your skills and experience to job descriptions; how and where to find job openings, skillfully answer difficult interview questions, discuss your strengths and weaknesses with confidence and professionalism, and deal with anxiety and stress, as well as gracefully recover from a "bad" interviewing experience. Chapter 12 will discuss how applying the concept of mental toughness to the process of looking for a job can help you remain optimistic and focused and successfully deal with frustration and rejection. Chapter 14 will show you how to quickly get yourself up to speed with the new technology by discussing job-searching techniques using Internet job boards, sending a resume by e-mail, preparing video resumes, and using such social networking sites as Facebook and LinkedIn to find job openings. Finally, Chapter 22 will outline strategies to help job seekers find employment in a tight economy.

The challenge for career changers of any age is how to stay relevant and successful in today's workplace. Although you cannot change the past, you can learn from the past and use that experience to improve your employment situation the second time around. Now is the time to begin the journey toward placing yourself in the career or work setting that will allow your strengths, talents, and experience to shine. It's time to reinvent yourself and reenergize your passion for life and living.

Chapter 1

MIDLIFE AND
RETIREMENT REDEFINED

Forty is the old age of youth; fifty the youth of old age.

Victor Hugo

In 1965, Elliott Jaques, a relatively unknown Canadian psychoanalyst and organizational consultant, published a paper in which he coined the term "midlife crisis." Jaques wrote that during the midlife period we come face-to-face with our limitations, our restricted possibilities, and our mortality.[1]

In his own life, Jaques did not seem to live with a sense of limitation. In the 38 years between the publication of that paper and his death in 2003 at age 86, he wrote 12 books; was a consultant to the U.S. Army, the Church of England, and a wide variety of companies; and married Kathryn Cason, with whom he founded a consulting company devoted to the dissemination of their ideas.

By the end of his first life, in his mid-forties, he had earned two doctorates, one in medicine and another in psychology. In his second life, Jaques became a truly independent thinker and created the concepts and theories for which he is most famous. Some of his most original ideas were formulated in the late 1990s, when he was in his late seventies and early eighties.

Midlife, or "Middle Age," is generally recognized as the years from 40 to 60 and is characterized by myths that cover everything from "midlife crisis" to "change-of-life" to "empty nest syndrome." Although the marketing industry affectionately refers to middle-aged individuals as the "Young Olds," some writers have suggested we call this extended period of life "Second Midlife," "Third Age,"[2] or the "Third Stage of Life."[3]

Individuals in midlife are made up of the Baby Boomers and Generation X. Members of the Baby Boom generation were born between 1946 and 1964. At their peak, Baby Boomers made up 46 percent of the workforce. In 2006, the oldest Baby Boomers reached 60 and began to retire.[4] Boomers are characterized as hard-working and loyal; they have tended to work at one company until they retire, have concentrated on moving up the corporate ladder, and have tied their identity to their jobs. This generation has been influenced by such social changes as the civil rights movement, the women's movement, and the Vietnam War and today has become a strong political force through such organizations as the American Association for Retired Persons (AARP).

Members of Generation X, or Gen Xers, were born between 1965 and 1980.[5] They are the children of the Baby Boom generation and have grown up in the shadow of high divorce rates, Vietnam, and Watergate. Generation X has been stereotyped by the popular media as hopelessly bored and aimless, but in reality Gen Xers are very focused, serious, and self-reliant. In fact, many of our Internet companies were born on the backs of Gen Xers who worked 80 hours a week and created the jobs.com world we live in today.

Gen Xers make up a much smaller percentage of the workforce, about 29 percent in 2005. Gen Xers want a career but will change jobs more frequently; and after watching their parents be let go after years of loyal service, they have little loyalty to any one company. Gen Xers are comfortable with racial diversity, embrace technology, are globally and civically minded, and are interested in non-traditional pursuits or "green" professions. Although members of this generation may take longer to find their true career calling, they are now in the peak years of their professional life and are coming into their own.

THE GRAYING OF THE AMERICAN WORKFORCE

In 2010, we will begin to see a large demographic shift in which the 65-and-older age group will increase and the 20–64 age group will decline.[6] As the Baby Boom generation ages, the number of workers 55 years and older will increase dramatically. In 2008, the Baby Boomer population was 44 to 62 years old. By 2018 almost all of the Boomers will be in the 55-and-older age group and are projected to make up nearly one-quarter of the total labor force.[7] While the number of older workers who stay in the workforce is expected to increase, it will remain significantly lower than those in the prime working age group (25–54 years of age), which will ultimately lower the total number of workers in the work-force and slow the growth of the labor force. In 2009 AARP commissioned a nationwide survey to determine the employment status of people 45 years or older. The survey examined whether people in this age group had lost jobs or sought new employment over the last 12 months. Twenty-seven percent of those aged 45–54 looked for a new job because of uncertainty about their current employment. Seventeen percent of respondents said they had postponed plans to retire. Twenty-seven percent of those in the age group approaching retirement age (ages 55–64) reported postponing plans to retire, and about one-fifth (19 percent) of this age group reported already being retired.[8] Despite the increasing number of older Americans reaching retirement age, a greater proportion of older Americans is expected to remain in the workforce instead of retiring. The increase in the continued employment rate of mature workers can be traced to a number of reasons:[9]

- People are living healthier and much longer lives than in the past, which increases the opportunity to work longer.
- Today's older workers are more educated than their past counterparts, which results in higher participation in the labor market.

- Loss of pension plans acts as an incentive to stay in the labor market for longer intervals. Retirement contribution plans that are based on an individual's and an employer's contribution are indifferent to the worker's retirement age. Hence, workers have more of an incentive to delay retirement so they can reap greater rewards in the future.
- In 2000, the full retirement age for Social Security began a scheduled increase. These changes were intended to discourage workers from retiring earlier.
- The high cost of health insurance and a decrease in health benefits have obligated many older workers to continue to work to keep their benefits or to go back to work after retirement.

RETIREMENT TRENDS

At the beginning of the century, two-thirds of American men over age 65 were still employed.[10] However, by 1950, just over 45 percent of American men over age 65 were employed. The labor force participation rate declined steadily until about 1985, then leveled off and even increased slightly, reaching 17.9 percent in 2000. A similar trend happened among men between the ages of 55 and 64. Their participation rate in the workforce fell from just under 87 percent in 1950 to almost 68 percent in 1985. The workforce participation rate of women age 65 and older has always remained relatively low, but the rate of women between ages 55 and 64 remaining in the workforce has increased sharply over the past several decades.

It appears that the trend toward early retirement has leveled off and has slowly begun to reverse.[11] Longer life expectancies and better medical treatment have made it possible for people who, in the past, would have had no choice but to leave the workforce to now make career changes and continue to work.[12] The oldest of the nation's 78 million Baby Boomers turned 62 in 2008. A 2004 study by AARP revealed that 79 percent of Boomers planned to remain in the workforce in some capacity past the traditional retirement ages of 62 to 65, partly because they enjoyed working but also because they needed the income.[13] A more recent 2007 survey showed that workers aged 45 to 74 want to stay on the job as long as their wants and needs are addressed.[14] This age group is motivated to continue to work for a variety of reasons, including having something to do, a sense of community or connectedness, and a sense of purpose. More than one-third identify "need the money" as the main financial motivator. Seventy percent prefer part-time work.

Although the Bureau of Labor Statistics stated that the labor force participation rate of women peaked in 1999, the number of women in the labor force is still projected to grow at a slightly faster rate than for men.[15] A 2006 MetLife survey revealed that women are more likely than men to work because they need the income to live on.[16] Single and divorced employees are almost twice as likely as those who are married to continue to work because they need the income to live on. Being able to afford health care in retirement is the concern for all employees, but it is far more important to women than men. Women are more concerned about outliving their retirement money (62 percent versus 42 percent for men).[17]

"I'm not ready to retire yet!" exclaimed Betty, a 61-year-old woman who was recently laid off by the insurance company she worked for as an executive secretary for 33 years. Too young for Social Security and not financially or emotionally ready to stop working, she updated her resume and found a part-time position with another insurance company.

CAREER TRENDS OVER THE LIFE SPAN

In general, as workers age they tend to shift from blue-collar to white-collar and services occupations and away from physically demanding occupations. Health is one variable that affects the ability of older individuals to work. In the 1940s and early 1950s, about 90 percent of new retirees cited poor health or a layoff as the reason they retired.[18] Less than 5 percent reported leaving because they wished to retire or enjoy more leisure. By the early 1980s, the reported reasons for leaving work began to shift. Nearly 50 percent of male retirees age 65 or older attributed their retirement to a desire to leave work, while only 20 percent cited poor health as a reason for retiring. Physical demands of work have lessened over the decades as our economy shifts from an industrial to a service economy that has allowed people with health limitations to remain working.

Retirement patterns also vary by industry. Manufacturing jobs are more likely to be unionized, which provides greater access to pension benefits and contributes to retirement decisions. More physically demanding jobs tend to lead to earlier retirements than do occupations that require less physical labor.

According to the Bureau of Labor Statistics best estimates, America will be short some 10 million skilled workers by 2011 because of the number of retiring Baby Boomers.[19] This shortage will cause what has been referred to as a "huge knowledge gap." As the Boomer generation approaches its retirement years, companies are starting to change the ways they define work. This outflow of competent workers also opens up many new job opportunities, even during a time when the economy is not growing.

Industries in the professional and technical groups will be greatly affected by Baby Boomer retirement, but educational services will be the most affected. Federal and state governments, as well as utility companies, have recently ramped up their recruiting efforts because of the impending shortages that will result from future retirements.

IMPACT OF THE AGING WORKFORCE ON THE WORKPLACE

One of the interesting ways that the aging workforce is changing the way we work is by bringing a measure of flexibility to the office. Companies are finding that employees in this age group require different work conditions. They are less interested in working long hours, less defined by their careers, and much more interested in part-time work. Telecommuting, job sharing, part-time work, and flex scheduling can be partially attributed to the Baby Boomer generation's influence. "Quality of life" has become a key phrase. Even members of the Generation X group are beginning to question their choice of careers and ponder how to balance career and family life. Instead of asking, "Where has my life gone?" as did their parents, this generation is asking, "Where do I want my life to go?"

"Phased retirement," a relatively new concept used by businesses, can take a variety of forms.[20] Some companies, like Stanley Consultants in Iowa, voted one of AARP's 2009 Best Employers for Workers Over 50, allow workers to gradually reduce their hours of employment without losing their benefits. Other companies use older workers as consultants, engage them as temporary, seasonal, or part-time employees, or allow them "leaves of absence" or job-sharing arrangements.

AGE EXPECTANCY

Humans are now living twice as long as previously expected to live. On September 11, 2009, the world's oldest person, 115-year-old African American Gertrude Baines, died in Los Angeles. The maximum life span for humans has been authenticated at 122 years with Frenchwoman Jeanne Calment's death in 1997.[21]

For persons living in industrialized countries, the average life span has risen from 35 or 40 years of age at the end of the 18th century to about twice that age today. The 2000 U.S. census revealed that the number of Americans over 65 years of age has more than doubled since 1950, largely because of advances in medical science and nutrition. In 2000, women outnumbered men about 3:2 in the over-65 age bracket; and in the over-85 age bracket, women outnumbered men by more than 2:1.[22]

The average life expectancy of humans in the United States is 79.2 years, according to a 2008 United Nations Population study, and is expected to increase to 83.3 years in 2050.[23] Women now live 81.4 years and men live 76.9 years. Heart disease and cancer are still the two deadliest conditions, but their death rates are dropping. Meanwhile, deaths from diseases mainly seen in elders, like Alzheimer's and Parkinson's disease, are on the rise.[24]

JOB PERFORMANCE AND THE OLDER WORKER

Although adults older than 55 show declines in several abilities, research correlating age with job performance finds almost no correlation between the two. One study found that the reaction time of typists declined with age, but their typing speed was the same as that of their younger counterpart because older typists tend to read ahead farther, thus readying themselves for typing material.[25]

Older workers can perform their jobs as effectively as their younger counterparts, especially when they (a) avoid suffering the physical and cognitive declines usually evident in their age group, (b) have a relatively high degree of experience and expertise in their job, (c) have some flexibility in adapting to job change, (d) are allowed to learn at their own pace, and (e) are trained by other senior managers who understand their unique needs.[26]

RETIREMENT REDEFINED

Retirement was never meant to be a long-term condition, just a well-deserved rest at the end of our careers. But as we live and work longer, the meaning of retirement has begun to evolve. The concept of Encore Career,[27] popularized by Marc Freedman, applies to people who have finished their midlife careers and who then engage in work that benefits society. "Work" and "Retirement" are periods of life that have never before coexisted—until now. The challenge for people approaching retirement age who want to continue to work will be to find a way to make the transition from a first career that shaped their identity for most of their adult lives to a second career that is new and yet fulfilling.

Unfortunately, there is no prescription for how to live the second or third stage of our lives. We cannot look to our parents for a model of how to retire successfully because our retirement will be influenced by better nutrition, better medical care, a more active lifestyle, more education, a different perspective of the world, and a greater number of resources. We will have to create a different type of retirement, one that is redefined in contemporary society and in light of our current and future economic marketplace. The whole concept of retirement is undergoing a fundamental change. Many of us will choose to adopt the old model of retirement by leaving work to spend our time playing golf, enjoying our grandchildren and great-grandchildren, or volunteering for our favorite social cause. But an equal number of us will want to continue to work full- or part-time, gain recognition, earn raises and promotions, be creative, and continue to be productive. One thing is for certain: whatever we end up doing in our "retirement" years will be much different than what our parents did during their retirement.

CAREER CHANGE IN MIDLIFE

Midlife may be a natural time to develop a new career plan because developmentally speaking, this is the time of life when individuals tend to reevaluate their lives. The departure of children, death of loved ones, and personal experience of illness cause us to confront our mortality for the first time. People in midlife are also dealing with a number of such transitional issues as empty nests, boomerang children, divorce, remarriage, grandchildren, caring for elderly parents, or career burnout.

Some people will experience a "midlife crisis" during their thirties or forties, but it is not as common or as traumatic as we've been led to believe. Psychologists describe midlife transition as a natural developmental stage that happens to many of us at some point in our lives, usually around age 40. This transition can include (a) discontentment or boredom with life or with your lifestyle, (b) feeling restless and wanting to do something completely different, (c) questioning decisions made years earlier and the meaning of life, and (d) confusion about who you are or where your life is going.[28]

Other people find their forties and fifties as a time of finally feeling settled and finding contentment within themselves. What separates midlife from 20 years earlier is that people in their forties and fifties tend to have developed into the people they were meant to be. One of the benefits of growing older is that people tend to care less about what others expect of them and look more deeply into what their inner desires are. Even if individuals in midlife are not completely sure what they want out of life, they certainly know what they *do not* want.

A 2009 AARP report examined the characteristics of workers who change careers late in life.[29] Using data from eight waves of the biennial Health and Retirement Study (1992–2006), the authors examined the extent and nature of career change by older workers and its consequences for later life employment. Their analyses indicate that nearly two-thirds of workers who change jobs (and 27 percent of all older workers) switch occupations. Late-life occupational change was more common among men because women were less likely to continue working if they left an employer in their fifties. Among those who do change jobs, however, women and men are equally likely to recareer. The new careers tend to offer more flexible employment arrangements, less stressful working conditions, and fewer managerial responsibilities. The research concludes by stating that later life career change seems to be an important part of the retirement process.

Interestingly, in my current career services position, I have seen an increase in the number of 55+ women interested in changing careers (an influence of the recent recession), women who are therefore indicating a desire to remain in the workforce.

Fear of aging affects our decision about career change. I've even heard students who were in their thirties talking about being "too old to change careers." It's all a matter of perception. I recently worked with a woman in her late fifties who previously enjoyed a very successful real estate business. Because of the real estate market bust, she is now looking for a second career because she is not mentally or financially ready to retire. She was not afraid of "starting over" because she did not view herself as old and did not see any reason to stop working.

Dr. Gene Cohen, author of *The Mature Mind: The Positive Power of the Aging Brain*,[30] describes midlife reevaluation as a more thoughtful focus on the meaning and quality of one's work, greater openness to new ideas and the complexities of life, an increased trust in one's intuitive feelings, and less impulsive reactions to situations in daily life. In this stage, we are truly able to find ourselves, renew our purpose in life, and feel refreshed and recharged. We have the luxury of hindsight, for we can look back and learn from the mistakes of our past and move forward in a new direction.

Recent economic conditions have made it necessary for people in their forties and fifties to go back to school, change jobs, or redesign their careers. We are seeing this trend in community colleges and in colleges and universities all across the country. In order to remain employable, middle-aged workers will have to assume more ownership of their career path and be responsible for updating their skills in order to remain competitive.

Consider this time in your life as an opportunity to shape the remainder of your life. Build the career you really want. As you work through this process, you will need to ask yourself some tough questions: How do I really want to spend the remaining 20 to 30 years of my life? Do I retool or retire? How much do I need to work to maintain my current quality of life? Do I adopt a new career or find a way to remain in touch with my profession but in a different role? What things matter most to me now? How will a career change impact my life? How will it affect my family?

Do not limit yourself by believing the stereotype that you are too old to start a new career. Although we do not know what challenges will present themselves in the future, we do know that we want the next phase of our lives to provide meaning, stability, security, creativity, enjoyment, and some degree of control over our lives. The second half of your life is waiting for you—and it is yours to create!

Chapter 2

So You Want to Change Your Career

Learn from the past. Deal with the present. Plan for the future.

Robert Morgan

It cannot be overestimated how job unhappiness can affect the rest of a person's life. Not only can a person's health be affected by the negative effects of stress and anger, but personal relationships suffer because unhappy workers come home miserable. When I changed my job, the first thing my husband noticed was that I did not complain (as much) when I came home from work. That's a pretty powerful statement.

Exercise 1: Wishing Exercise

1. What would it feel like to enjoy your job so much that you actually woke up looking forward to going to work?
2. On a scale of 1 to 10, circle the number that best represents how badly you want to change your career.

    1   2   3   4   5   6   7   8   9   10

3. Was there something you always wanted to do but never had the chance? Be a teacher, an artist, or own your own business, for example?
4. If you could do anything right now, what would it be?
5. When you catch yourself thinking, "I wish I could go home" or "I wish I was [somewhere else]," where would you rather be? What would you rather be doing?
6. Do you feel as if something is missing from your life? What is missing?
7. What do you want to accomplish in your lifetime? What do you want to be remembered for?
8. How would a career change improve your life?

Steven

Steven was a news reporter for a small radio and television station. After working for several years, he realized he was just not going to make enough money to support himself and his family. Although he enjoyed the broadcast communications industry, he was tired of the erratic hours and low pay typical of the radio business. So he got a job as a salesman. Several years later, he met his wife, Donna, who was a physical therapist. Steven had always had an interest in health care, and as he grew older he wanted to do something that made a difference in other people's lives. After seeing how much his wife enjoyed her work and was able to help people on a daily basis, Steven decided to go back to school, part-time, for his registered nursing degree. Today, he is in a career not only that he loves but that allows him the flexibility of working second shift so he or his wife can be home with their children while the other is working, eliminating the need to put their children in daycare.

FINDING MEANING IN WORK

Work means different things to different people. Yale researcher Amy Wrzesniewski describes three distinct orientations people have toward work:[1]

- *Work as a job.* Seeing work as a source of income. Satisfaction comes from hobbies and relationships outside work. Holding a job to support a family or to fund one's hobbies is an example.
- *Work as a career.* Seeing work as a source of advancement, prestige, and status. Job satisfaction comes primarily from continuing advancement. People who see work as a career will often dedicate extraordinary amounts of time and energy to their work.
- *Work as a calling.* Seeing work as a calling, some people derive satisfaction from the work itself because they believe it contributes to the greater good. People with this orientation tend to experience more meaning from working.

All three orientations were found at all levels in an employment hierarchy. Wrzesniewski also found that people who consider their jobs "callings" experience greater life satisfaction.

CHANGE YOUR JOB OR CHANGE YOUR OCCUPATION?

There is a difference between changing your job (you like the work but not the company you work for or the people you work with) and changing your occupation (you do not like the actual work that you do). The former can be improved by changing employers or industries. The latter can only be changed by moving to a different career field. Is your current company not taking advantage of the breadth and depth of your skills? If one of your reasons for wanting to change careers is because you have no room to advance, is there another company within the same career that would offer a better salary or rewards? Or are you at the top of your job level and need to look at a career that offers more income potential? If you still enjoy doing accounting work but not for the company or boss you work for, then changing employers may be the answer. If you have been a teacher for the last 15 years and are tired of the latest educational rhetoric, have come to dislike your school system, and find that you do not enjoy working with children as much as you used to, a career change may be in order. However, if you still enjoy teaching but do not like the administration or the philosophy of your school district, then finding a different employer or a different type of educational setting may do the trick.

Someone who has been working as an emergency room nurse for the last eight years and is burned out from the stress and is experiencing physical symptoms of exhaustion needs to determine if he or she still enjoys the basic elements of nursing. That person's choice would be either to stay in the nursing field in a new capacity, perhaps in a different setting as a school nurse or nursing instructor at a college, or to make a 360-degree switch to another career where work proceeds at a slower pace or the care is for people in less critical situations.

The Reasons People Change Careers

Let's look at the some of the reasons why people want to change careers. Some people no longer feel motivated to go to work, perhaps because they have advanced in their career as far as they can and are no longer challenged by the day-to-day activities or they are burned out from intensive client or customer interaction. Others feel their skills and creativity are not being utilized or they are ready to take on new challenges, want to assume a higher level of responsibility, or are looking for a position more rewarding in terms of salary and benefits. Some people like their jobs but find that the position just does not pay enough to support a family or the type of lifestyle they want. Sometimes changes in technology, the economy, or the industry they have worked in (e.g., manufacturing, the dot.-com industry) mean their jobs have changed or vanished, and as a consequence there are no longer any job opportunities.

Many people in midlife discover that their values and life circumstances have changed from when they first began their careers. What was once so important does not seem quite so critical anymore. They may have matured, developed a different set of priorities, or have had a major life-altering experience that has affected their outlook on life. For example, you may have been single when you first began working and thrived on a fast-paced, deadline-based work environment filled with frequent traveling and lucrative promotions. Now that you have a family, however, this type of lifestyle no longer works for you. The question now becomes how to balance a career and family life. Others may have chosen careers based on income potential, power, and status but now find their value system changing as they grow older. They find that the old rewards and perks no longer motivate them. Many people in midlife begin to rethink work and redefine their purpose in life, and as a consequence they look at the world differently.

According to Gene Cohen,[2] the first step in midlife reevaluation is characterized by deep introspection and a renewed search for meaning. The second phase is liberation, when you realize you have nothing more to lose and are free to pursue your passions.

Some individuals seek to go beyond their high-profile careers to spend their time volunteering or focusing on alleviating the problems of our world by working in schools, in health care, or as social entrepreneurs. The experts call this phase practical idealism and pragmatic creativity, which is a blend of work and personal satisfaction that sustains the individual and gives back to the community.[3]

The most dangerous reason for changing your job or career is that you think the grass is greener on the other side. Are you running away from a bad situation? Unless you identify what you are running away from, you run the risk of running into another poor employment choice.

Exercise 2: Career Change Reasons

Place a check beside each reason that describes why you want to make a career change.

1. ___My life, my values, or my goals have changed.
2. ___My job is not rewarding enough.
3. ___There is no room to advance.
4. ___My values clash with the company's values or philosophy.
5. ___I want to do something more meaningful.
6. ___I want a job that lets me help others.
7. ___I want to enjoy what I'm doing.
8. ___I am not using my creativity or my skills to their full potential.
9. ___I've done this for the last 15 years and do not want to do it anymore.
10. ___My work is boring.
11. ___I am experiencing job burnout.
12. ___My job is too stressful, or it contains too much responsibility.
13. ___I'm not earning enough money.
14. ___The job outlook in my field has worsened.
15. ___My job requires too much travel.
16. ___I hate the hours.
17. ___I do not like or get along with my coworkers, my boss, or the company I work for.
18. ___I do not enjoy the daily tasks of my job.
19. ___The work is too hard on my body.
20. ___I do not feel ethical, safe, or secure in what I'm doing.
21. ___I know I can do something better with my life.
22. ___I just can't stand it here anymore.
23. ___I like the people I work with but not the company or the daily job tasks.
24. ___I have more talents than this job is using.
25. ___I could run this company myself, or I'd rather be the boss.

If you checked **Questions 1–7, 20, and 23**, then you have a clash of work values. Work values are the aspects of your job that you find personally meaningful and rewarding and are a leading cause of satisfaction or dissatisfaction at work.

Work values may be characteristic of the job itself, such as the amount of direct contact with people, or they may be such byproducts of the profession, as the opportunity to travel to other parts of the country on business. If you value being able to do precise work or help other people improve their lives and are not in a job that allows you to fulfill those values, then your work will become meaningless and sterile over time. Identify those values that are most important, or essential, in a job and separate out those that may be met outside of work.

Work values also have to do with the amount of personal meaning you assign to your work and what your role at work means to you. This ultimately all comes down to perception. One person can view cleaning as a respectful and needed profession with no loss of self-esteem, whereas another might view cleaning as a menial profession. Pretend for a moment that you cleaned houses for a living. Would you perceive yourself as "someone who cleans houses" or as a "cleaning lady or man"?

Do you identify yourself with your profession or with the company you work for? How important is it to have a strong professional identity? Think about how you perceive your current job, and then think about how others perceive you in your job. Next, compare those perceptions to how you would like to perceive or be perceived in your new career. The insight will not only provide you with valuable information about yourself but also give you some direction about your future choice of career.

Many people cite "no possibility of advancement" as a reason for wanting to change jobs or careers. People who possess serious drive and ambition find it very frustrating to hit a career ceiling. Some people become so bored at work that they have already mentally checked out of their jobs. Again, determine whether it's the job or the career that no longer contains any room for advancement. Then, begin making plans to change your job or career before your attitude and productivity decrease to the point where you risk damaging a potential reference source.

Questions 3, 13–14 deal with the financial aspects of working. Some people are more motivated by money than others. If you are not making enough to support your family or to provide you with the type of lifestyle you would like to have, you will want to search for a career or industry that can provide more financial stability or more earning potential.

Question 19 deals with physical demands of the job. Warehouse work, production jobs, and many trade occupations will involve considerable physical wear and tear on the body, whereas construction, landscaping, and surveying professions will also require working out in the elements. A supervisory position in a customer service–based industry is going to have a work environment that is not only heavy in customer contact but is also quota-driven, with a high level of activity. The advertising or marketing industry is often characterized by a fast pace, teamwork, and adherence to deadlines. Such work as management positions between parent and subsidiary companies may involve frequent overnight travel. Commissioned sales positions are going to be financially unstable because of the lack of a predictable paycheck at the end of each month. Each can be a source of motivation for some people or a source of stress for others.

If you enjoy your career but prefer a job with less travel or fewer erratic hours, you may want to consider working for a more family-friendly company or seek a career that offers a more flexible schedule or summers off to spend time with your kids (e.g., education). However, the work schedule is only one of several factors to be considered when choosing a new career. I would not suggest selecting a teaching career solely because you may have your summers off if you do not like working with children. Occupations contain a whole package of factors that need to be considered when trying to find one that best matches your skills, values, and personal requirements.

Questions 11 and 12 relate to the physical and emotional reactions you have toward your job. Do you get a headache or a tight feeling in the pit of your stomach when you think about work? Listen to your body—it's giving you clues about your discomfort, which is usually caused by an internal or external source of stress. The stress may be originating from pressure coming from your boss, expected sales quotas, level of responsibility, consequences of decisions, customer demands, lack of staffing, or an overwhelming amount of customer service. You may need to find a job or profession that has more traditional hours, operates at a slower pace, provides more autonomy, or has less responsibility. The other possibility is to analyze your personal operating style. Some of your stress may be a result of your inability to delegate responsibility or say no to requests. If you are willing to work too long, take on too much responsibility, or have difficulty setting appropriate boundaries, handling conflict, or resolving disputes, the position may not be the best fit for your personality. Try to determine whether it is your occupation that's stressful or just your particular place of employment. If the answer is your place of employment, then a job change, rather than a career change, may do the trick.

Physical discomfort on the job can also result from relationship issues in your office. If you checked **Question 17**, there may be some discord between you and your boss or confrontation between coworkers. If your boss is friendly and supportive but ineffective—or a pain but generally fair—then the decision to stay or leave comes down to a matter of personal choice and tolerance for that type of boss. If you are being held back by your boss, however, then it's time to leave. Coworkers, on the other hand, are another issue. At every company, there will always be people you enjoy working with and those you do not. Remember that you are not required to like everyone you work with—just work with them. Ultimately, the issue comes down to your level of patience and personal tolerance of those around you and how important it is to you to work with people you like.

If you checked **Question 4**, your physical discomfort may also stem from an ethical dilemma. Is your company involved in something unethical or illegal? Are you required to "stretch the truth" to customers? Are you overseeing finances that have the potential to turn into another Enron situation? Your level of discomfort will depend on your personal moral compass and how much you are willing to risk your professional integrity and reputation for a reward you may or may not receive.

If you checked **Question 24**, you may be feeling underappreciated. Is the source of that feeling coming from the way a supervisor is treating you? Is it a result of the level of your job responsibilities? Do the answers to these questions mean that you desire advancement or recognition?

If your work is "too boring" (**Question 10**), what makes it boring? What would make your job more exciting? Is your career boring or is it your particular job? Are the job duties or position level too elementary for your skill level? If you have the skills to be in charge and are doing administrative support tasks, then your work is too elementary and you need to seek a position with greater responsibility. You may need to go back to school to earn a degree that would qualify you for a position with greater responsibility.

If you checked **Question 8**, "I am not using my creativity or my skills to their full potential," you might function better in a position with more autonomy, responsibility, or leadership role. If you do not currently have the skills, experience, or education to qualify for such a position, then you will want to initiate a strategic career plan that will allow you to reach that goal. Career planning will be discussed further in Chapter 9.

If you checked **Question 25** or are "feeling bored" or "have no place to advance," it may be time to for you to start your own business and be in charge of your own destiny. Recognize that running your own company is not as easy as it sounds. While it's true that you can take all the credit if you are successful, it is also equally true that when things go wrong, you will have to assume all the blame. Try to determine whether your dissatisfaction stems from factors that can be changed with a job or career change, or are indicative of your true desire to work at home or "for yourself."

A mismatch between personality type and the requirements of the job can also result in an unhappy work situation. If you are a quiet person who prefers to stay out of the limelight, then a highly visible, first-line-of-contact position in the public eye is going to be very uncomfortable. Likewise, if you are an outgoing person who thrives on social contact, then a job as a computer software programmer is not going to do it for you.

If you find yourself saying, "I hate my job," or "I just can't stand it here anymore," or "I want to do something different, but I do not know what it is," you may be reacting on a purely emotional level. Try to figure out specifically what it is about your job that you hate so you can identify what to look for in a future job.

Understanding what motivates you and how you make decisions in your life is useful information that can help you to avoid making another poor choice in the future. Keep in mind that the decision to change jobs or careers will have a significant impact on other areas of your life. Be cautious and patient during this process, and make sure you are leaving for the right reasons.

CHANGING CAREERS IN MIDLIFE

Midlife is an ideal time to re-create your life. You have the benefit of looking back on what you did before and observing who you have become today. Most people in midlife are ready to take charge of their lives and head in a new direction.

The goal of any career change is to move to a more enjoyable employment situation. A career change can be a dramatic change from one occupation to a totally unrelated one, or a small step such as changing roles at your current place of employment.

Too often, people dismiss pursuing their passions and dreams because to do so they might need additional schooling or because they feel they will be throwing away the years they invested in graduate school or the time they have spent in their current careers. The reality is that you are never completely starting over. You are the culmination of your work, education, and life experience. What you accomplished in your first career(s) will only serve to contribute to what you do in the future. Think of it as a layering effect—building knowledge, skills, and experience layer by layer, each one contributing to the next over the years. Everything you have learned is a transferable skill that can be used in the future in ways that are unimaginable to you at the present time.

Unplanned Career Change

Unfortunately, in today's economy many people are forced to make an *involuntary* career change because of plant closures, downsizings, or layoffs. These individuals are faced with the difficult task of having to reinvent themselves and their future.

Karla

Karla, a former retail store manager, talks about the day she found out she was one of several managers being downsized.

"It was devastating! I worked there for 12 years and loved my job! I felt like I had put my heart and soul into that job, and suddenly it was snatched away! After many months of desperate soul-searching, a friend suggested I apply for a teaching position at a local college. Even though I didn't have any formal teaching experience, they hired me as an adjunct, and later I was able to move into a permanent teaching position."

Nine years later, Karla is still teaching at that college and is a favorite professor among her students in the Small Business Management program.

Sometimes people are forced to change their careers because of an injury or accident that leaves them unable to perform their job tasks. A construction worker who injures his back or a court reporter who develops carpal tunnel syndrome suddenly finds himself searching for a new career because he can no longer lay asphalt or transcribe court proceedings.

According to the 2009 CareerBuilder survey of 807 workers who were laid off from full-time jobs within the last 12 months, 38 percent of workers said they found work in a field that differed from their previous employment, and 70 percent of those said they really enjoy the new opportunity.[4]

"I'm thinking about regret," Natalie said as she began to tear up in my office. "I should have done this so much sooner; if I did then, I'd be that much further along now." Whether or not that is true is something we'll never know, but my guess is that she had had a different set of priorities, interests, and issues at that time in her life that influenced the decisions she made. Given the circumstances, she probably made the best decision for her at the time. Natalie was still raw with grief over losing her job. It will take some time for her grief to subside and allow her to view her situation with the proper perspective.

The upside of recession, if there is one, is that it may have given you the chance to write that book, spend more time with the kids, or turn a passionate hobby into a business. When you were employed, you may have thought it too risky to make a career change or too expensive to go back to school. Perhaps you were content with the money you were making and did not want to risk a change because things were going well. Now that has changed. As awful as unemployment is, many people look back on being laid off as the best thing that ever happened to them because it forced them to rethink their goals and priories. After a period of soul-searching, they often find new work that is more fulfilling, lucrative, or both.

Tom

I worked with Tom, a married warehouse supervisor who was laid off after 17 years. Tom had no education beyond high school. Since he wanted to do something other than sit around collecting his unemployment checks, he began checking out college incentive programs for displaced workers. Tom had a cushion—unemployment plus severance package. Also, his wife owned her own business, so they had a second income. Now Tom had time to think about what he wanted to do in future. He confided that he had not been happy in his warehouse job, and for about the last three years he had actually dreaded going to work each day. The up side of being unemployed was that he was able to spend time with his kids. Previously, he had always been on second shift, so he had never had time to spend with family. Now he did and was making the most of it. Tom viewed his unemployment as a positive event because it compelled him to do something different about his work situation.

Unemployment is the great equalizer and tends to change a person's perspective. Maybe it's the motivation you need to make that career change today!

MOVING BEYOND FEAR OF CHANGE

It's perfectly normal to have some self-doubt when going through a career change. Having a healthy concern about quitting one's job or going back to school is useful because it compels you to plan before you leap. Too much worry, however, may cause you to remain stuck and immobile.

All change, even positive change, is going to feel uncomfortable at first because you are leaving the safety of the familiar and venturing into the unknown. However, there are ways to make the transition seem less risky and less overwhelming. One strategy is to thoroughly research your new career and what the change will entail. The second strategy is to take the process one step at a time. Some people make the transition from their current job to a new career field slowly over a period of years. They may spend time thinking and planning, or they may slowly ease their way into their future career by volunteering in their new field after normal working hours, taking a part-time job, or working freelance assignments in their field(s) of interest, using their vacation time to explore other industries or career fields, or taking college courses online or at night or on weekends.

Some people find that they need a "push" from a precipitating event, like the death of a family member or unemployment, to jump-start their career change plans.

Joan

Joan had a rewarding career helping adult students in a single-parent program be successful in college. When rumors started swirling that the grant funding the program might be in danger of not being renewed the following year, she began thinking about what she might do if she found herself unemployed. One thought that kept coming back to her was how she had always wanted to be a nurse. Joan switched her major to education (which she enjoyed) because she would have had to live away from home to attend nursing school. The thoughts pulled at her enough that she finally decided to take some action by brushing up on some requisite pre-nursing courses while she was still employed and receiving tuition reimbursement from her employer, and in three years she was able to graduate with an RN in nursing and begin her new career.

Too many people box themselves into hopeless situations by limiting what they can do with "should" and "can't" statements. With a little problem solving and creativity, there is a way to accomplish anything you set your mind to. Try asking yourself, "What would happen if I succeeded?" "What would my life be like?" "What would it feel like to actually like my job?"

How much control do you believe you have over your career? Do you believe you have the power to choose what you want to do, or do you feel that you are a victim of circumstances? Perhaps you believe the economy is too bad to change careers or that you'll never be able to find a job in a new career. One thing is for sure, unless you are able to change your attitude, alter your perspective, or move to a different job within your company, your situation will probably not improve. You have more control over your work situation that you realize.

Finally, if you are concerned that you do not have enough time, at your age, to make a change, consider that many of us still have a third, a half, or more of our adult lives left to live. We are likely to have a lot more "time" left to make the change than we think.

To Change or Not to Change Careers

Although this book is written for those who want to make a career change, each potential career changer must make the decision whether or not to leave his or her career path. Therefore, this book would be incomplete if it did not include a discussion of ways to make your current career more tolerable. If you find that the strategies suggested here are successful in making your current career more satisfying, then you may find that you will have to change only your job, not your career.

If you really enjoy your job and the work you do but cannot stand your boss, there are a number of ways to approach the situation: (a) try to change your attitude toward that person; (b) wait for your boss to move up or out; (c) try to diffuse the situation, have a frank discussion with your boss, or use someone else to act as a mediator to try to improve situation. However, you may be in a situation where too much time has passed, there is too much bitterness, or the relationship has been damaged beyond repair. As with the couple who have been in a bad marriage for too long, there is no more hope of salvaging the relationship except through divorce. Work on what you can, and change what is in your power to change. If that is not enough to improve the situation, you may have to make the decision to leave.

Does your current situation involve a well-paying job that provides a comfortable living for your family, including a large house, car, or private college education for your children? Are you trapped in a lifestyle that is too good or has become too essential to give up? If this is your situation, but you are still unhappy, then your unhappiness is telling you that this lifestyle is not as ideal as you were led to believe. Can you identify what is missing from your life? Can you downsize any part of your lifestyle or find another career path that allows you to earn a similar salary but with fewer hours or less stress? If the recent economic meltdown has taught us anything, it's the value of living within our means and finding such simple pleasures close to home as backyard barbeques with family and friends.

Some people decide they can live with a less-than-ideal work situation because the benefits they gain allow them to maintain a certain lifestyle. Others realize that their current profession is not really all that bad, that all they need is a fresh perspective or a way to increase the number of enjoyable tasks at work and decrease the less enjoyable ones. Others choose to express their real passions on weekends or evenings. If you are close to retirement, you may be able to tolerate your current situation for a little while longer. If you have been suddenly laid off, then you will need to decide whether to retire or retool. In either case, this is a personal decision and the only right answer is the one that works best for you. So determine whether a change is right for you at this point in your life. There are some inherent risks involved in making any kind of change, but there are ways to minimize the risk. If you decide to change your career, your next task will be to develop a plan to reach your new career goal, a topic that will be discussed in Chapter 9. On the other hand, if you have determined that a change is not right for you, develop a strategy to obtain what you want or need that will enrich your life outside of work.

Ten Questions You Should Ask Yourself Before Changing Careers

Consider the following questions well before you make any transition from your current job or career:

1. Am I dissatisfied with my career or only with my job or employer?
2. Do I feel I could use more of my abilities and skills in another occupation?

3. Do I know where my career interests lie?

4. Do I know what type of environment I'd prefer to work in?

5. What would I be giving up and what would I be gaining by changing careers?

6. How important are my current job's security, seniority, retirement, and health benefits? How will these benefits be affected by a career change?

7. Do I have the time, money, energy, and resources to make a career change or to develop the skills needed for a new career?

8. How will a career change impact my family? Is my family or significant other supportive of my change?

9. Have I developed a list of short-term and long-term goals and the steps needed to successfully complete my career change?

10. Am I ready to make a career change today? If not today, when I do I think I will be ready?

Your answers to these questions reflect your readiness to transition to a new career. You may find that after reflecting, you are prepared to start your change today. Or you may realize that it would be better or more prudent to begin your transition in three, five, or ten years down the road. There are no wrong answers. It's all about finding the best solution for you.

Chapter 3

FIND THE RIGHT JOB FIT

The first duty of a human being is to assume the right functional relationship to society—more briefly, to find your real job, and do it.

Charlotte Perkins Gilman

The previous chapter asked you to identify why you want to make a career change. This chapter goes a step further and asks you to identify the attributes of your ideal job. To find a new career that will more closely match your strengths and work style, you have to know what you are looking for. This means you need to understand how you best function in the workplace and what work settings and environments will bring out your strengths.

YOUR ATTITUDE TOWARD WORK

Let's first begin by looking at what work means to you in general. Think back to your childhood and try to recall the messages you received about work from your parents, family members, or friends. In my family, it was very important to get a good education so you did not end up in a so-called dead-end job. That type of labeling implies that accomplishment is important and that some jobs are considered better than others.

Now examine your current attitudes about having a career or job. Are there any similarities or differences in your current attitude compared with past attitudes? Do you need to make any changes in your attitude toward work? How much importance are you placing on your job? Is your career only one aspect of your life, or does your life revolve around your career? How does your work define you? Do you want your work to be a *job*, a *career*, or a *calling*?

Exercise 1: Attitudes

1. How do you feel when you think about your job?
2. How do you feel when you arrive at work? Apprehensive? Sick? Happy? Excited? Thoughtful?
3. How do you feel when you are going home at the end of the day?
4. What do you like best about your current (or most recent) job?
5. What do you not like about your current job?

Exercise 2: Finding the Deeper Meaning

1. When driving to work I feel _____ because I
   _____. When I'm at work I feel _____
   because _____
   and that means_____.
2. I hate it when my boss does or says_____ because that makes
   me feel_____.

Think about a job you really enjoyed. Why was it enjoyable? What did you do? How did you feel? Why? Then think about a job you hated and ask yourself what made it so unbearable? The people? The atmosphere? The work itself? What does this information tell you about yourself, your values, and your beliefs?

Think about when you were most satisfied, when you were dissatisfied, and write down the common words that keep coming up. What is your preferred work style? Do you work better with a team of people or alone? Do you thrive on completing projects or meeting deadlines, or do you prefer a slower, more predictable routine? Many of these preferences are based on your personality and the way you approach working.

If you are having trouble pinpointing your work style, there are several standardized assessments, like the *Myers-Briggs Type Indicator*, that can help you define these traits. You can also identify your personal work style by observing your own behavior in your current and past jobs.

Exercise 3: Discovering Ideal Work Elements

1. What type of work excites or inspires you?
2. What type of work bores or does little to motivate you?
3. What type of boss do you prefer to work for?
4. What type of management style brings out the best in you?
5. What type of office environment do you work best in?
6. When are you at your best or on your "A" game?
7. When are you not at your best?
8. How much flexibility, autonomy, or direction do you need?
9. What are your triggers or buttons (things that get under your skin)?
10. What stifles your creativity or ambition?
11. What motivates you?
12. What do you need for a reward system?

When asked to identify the essential elements of their ideal job, 91 percent of AARP survey respondents named the "chance to use your skills and talents" and 75 percent named the "opportunity to learn something new."[1] Write down your ideal elements in a job.

Exercise 4: Work Values

Building on the discussion of work values in Chapter 2, consider that work values are often the core components of our work, for they provide satisfaction, meaning, a sense of accomplishment, and fulfillment on our jobs. Although values can be satisfied in a variety of life roles, work that directly contradicts our values, (as might personal ethical violations) or that is not a good match to who we are will lead to major dissatisfaction. Begin by examining the following list of values and checking which of them you hold.

1. _____Helping others.
2. _____Being in control or being the boss.
3. _____Being independent, making your own decisions.
4. _____Taking risks, doing exciting things.
5. _____Being physically active.
6. _____Performing tasks in an ordered, efficient manner.
7. _____Performing intellectually stimulating tasks.
8. _____Being alone with your own thoughts or having quiet time.
9. _____Having variety in your job.
10. _____Being creative or original.
11. _____Working with your hands or using your hands to build, repair, groom, or improve things.
12. _____Being recognized for your accomplishments.
13. _____Performing for or entertaining others.
14. _____Being accepted by others or belonging to a group.
15. _____Acquiring such things as money, property, or clients.

When you are researching career possibilities, use these results to find a career that contains the features that best compliment your work style, personality, and values.

People who tend to prefer a quiet, reflective environment in order to think and plan would not do well in an environment characterized by chaos, constant interruption, and unpredictability. People perform best when placed in a work setting that allows their strengths to dominate and flourish. Some careers lend themselves better to certain personality types than others. Salespeople, in general, need to be comfortable going out and talking to people, often taking the initiative to meet people they have never met before, and spending most of their time talking, demonstrating products, or being persuasive. Laboratory technicians, in contrast, need to be comfortable working in a quiet, clinical, or sterile environment with limited people contact and maximum attention to procedures, steps, and detail.

The example I often use with students is the accounting career. If you enjoy accounting but are a person who needs to have daily contact with people, then you may want to become an accounting teacher or professor or a CPA in private practice who meets with a variety of clients each day. On the other hand, if you prefer a more behind-the-scenes environment with less people or customer contact, then a position in a corporate or educational business office where you have opportunity to work in the privacy of your office may be the ideal place for you.

What most people do not realize is that there are many methods and ways of accomplishing the same job and that work environments can be tailored, to some degree, to optimizing your work style. Developing a Web site, for example, can be completed in a small, quiet office setting where you can consult with people as needed but then spend the reminder of your time behind your computer with the door closed; or the site can be created in an open office environment where you bounce ideas off other people and engage in a collaborative exercise. There is not necessarily one right way to perform a job or task as long as you can produce quality results.

Exercise 5: Design Your Ideal Job

Now it's time for you to design your ideal job. Incorporate your priority list of work values, and consider the physical space, social aspects, intellectual challenge, and other intangibles that would make up an ideal career or job. Then, use that information to search for a career that most closely matches your requirements. Realize that rarely are we able to find a job or career that is perfect in every way, but it should contain those elements that you feel are critical to creating meaning, enjoyment, and success.

My ideal job would be in the _____industry. I would work in an (setting or environment) _____. My day would consist of doing _____. I would work or interact with (people, equipment, materials, etc.) _____.
I would be (supervised, independent, have no boss) _____ and would have an office or work environment that looked like

_____.
I would enjoy this position because I would be able to _____ and use my _____ (skills, education, and work experience). I feel I would be successful in this position because _____.

A job should be satisfying at least 75 percent of the time. Some people have described a job as being like a relationship. There are good aspects and bad aspects to every job. You need to decide which ones are the most important or essential and which ones are too annoying to live with.

Chapter 4

TELL ME ABOUT YOURSELF

Don't tell me how hard you work. Tell me how much you get done.

James Ling

TELL ME ABOUT YOURSELF

"So, tell me about yourself," is a deceptively simple question often used by interviewers to "break the ice" but is very difficult for most people to answer. How would you answer that question? (Hint: "Uhhh" is *not* the correct response.)

"Tell me about yourself" is not a social question—it is a professional inquiry about your educational background and your accumulated work experience. It is not about your age, your hobbies, the state of the union, or your latest eBay purchase. Being able to answer this question effectively requires that you distill your best strengths, knowledge, and work skills into a few well-formulated, concise sentences. Your response to the "tell me about yourself" question is a critical component of your job search campaign and provides the foundation for preparing a resume, inquiring about job openings, making new networking contacts, introducing yourself to a potential employer, or effectively highlighting your qualifications during an interview.

IDENTIFY YOUR SKILLS

If you wanted to sell a classic car, you would describe the *features* of your car that you felt would appeal to a potential buyer. The same holds true for people. Instead of listing the number of miles (even though it may *feel* that way), you would emphasize your years of experience; instead of listing the leather interior and the amount of horsepower in the engine, you would emphasize your knowledge, attitude, behavior, skills, or ability to make the company money.

Job skills are the abilities you learned from work experience or academic preparation that are needed to perform a specific job. Possessing job skills is what makes you attractive to an employer. An example of a job skill in the dental assisting field is taking an x-ray.

Many people have difficulty distinguishing *job duties* from *job skills*. Duties are the activities you perform on the job, such as generating reports, helping coordinate a trade show, or providing desktop support. Skills are the tools and techniques you use to accomplish these tasks, such as knowing how to program in C++, having written or oral communication abilities, or managing the billing department in an engineering firm. Employers usually organize job skills around different areas of expertise. These areas can include communication skills, ability to problem solve or troubleshoot, understanding the human relations aspect of jobs, leadership abilities, or such technical skills as computer programming, graphic design, or laboratory techniques. A troubleshooter can usually easily identify areas that need improvement and create and implement plans to boost work performance. A planner can be someone who takes an analytical approach to work and has past examples of figuring out ways to improve the work environment. Leadership can mean training other employees, leading teams, and providing motivation. It can also mean you have taken the initiative to start new programs or improve your work environment. Being able to work independently is an excellent job skill to possess. If you do have managerial or supervisory experience, these transfer very well to other types of work and should definitely be included on a resume.

Commonly Used Skills in the Workplace

Consider the following examples of commonly used workplace skills.

Active Listening	Operations Analysis
Critical Thinking	Operation and Control
Design	Organization
Equipment Maintenance	Persuasion
Installation	Problem Solving
Instruction and Training	Programming
Judgment and Decision Making	Quality Control Analysis
Management of Financial Resources	Repairing
Management of Material Resources	Science
Management of Personnel Resources	Social Perceptiveness
Mathematics	Speaking
Monitoring	Systems Analysis
Negotiation	Time Management
Troubleshooting	Writing

Skills may be implied through education or may be acquired through work experience. A master's degree in Library Science (which is the recognized level of education to be a professional librarian), for example, assumes that the degree holder knows about the ethics, values, and foundational principles of libraries and understands collection management; information systems and technology; research methods; preservation; reference; and library administration. Likewise, the skill set for an administrative assistant would include answering the telephone, taking dictation, scheduling appointments, preparing business correspondence, generating reports or PowerPoint presentations, making travel arrangements, scheduling meetings, or coordinating special functions or events. All these duties imply mastery (or at least some level of experience) of a set of skills. For example, being able to answer the switchboard implies that the worker knows proper telephone etiquette, customer service, and good communication skills. Dictation implies excellent word-processing ability as well as the ability to listen and accurately transcribe notes from a live or recorded delivery method and then prepare an electronic or paper letter, report, or document from that transcription in a professionally approved format (legal, business, or medical). Dictation, like transcription, is a skill set that not everyone possesses. If an employer is looking for someone with this skill set and you have this skill, then you are directly in contention for the position to be filled.

TRANSFERABLE SKILLS

Transferable job skills are skills you develop throughout your life that can be applied to a variety of situations. An example of a transferable skill is the ability to prioritize multiple requests. As a career changer, you have an extensive background of transferable skills from your past positions that can be brought forward and used in your future position. The broader your experience, the more skills you have, and the more value you bring to a company.

Such transferable skills as knowing how to answer the phone properly, scheduling appointments, managing an office, or conducting a meeting can be used in a manufacturing plant, the admissions office at a college, or a doctor's office. Likewise, the basic techniques of teaching a class are the same whether you are teaching chemistry to college students, teaching new computer skills to office employees at an insurance company, or training a new employee how to use the cash register at a convenience store. The difference between these jobs is not in the skills required to do them but in the setting and the changed educational context.

As a career changer, your task is to identify your transferable skills and package them in way that will appeal to an employer in a different field. Some job skills lend themselves more readily to transferring to other jobs without further education than others. A sales professional (who has experience doing product promotion and marketing) can easily transition to a job as a corporate trainer, a real estate agent, an educational sales consultant, a college recruiter for the human resources department, and even to a supervisory position for a large telemarketing or customer service department.

The following are examples of transferable skills commonly associated with a particular job that can be transferred to a position in another field. For example, a teacher can transfer his or her communication and presentation skills to a position in public relations or sales.

Teaching: Communication skills, deliver presentations, use multimedia, develop coursework, work with diverse people, appreciate differences, convey information, present material, and assess learning or skill mastery.

Coordinated a project, worked on a team, or belonged to a committee: Teamwork, plan events, arrange schedules, assign duties, coordinate volunteers, multi-task, meet deadlines, use diplomacy, delegate responsibilities, and take a project from start to completion.

Designing: Conceptualize, use creativity, manage resources and mediums, cost out a project, and develop plans.

Coaching: Teach, organize activities, inspire or teach teamwork, motivate others, and present information.

Sales: Teach, recruit, develop strong partnerships and working relationships, elicit cooperation, motivate others to act, marketing, public relations, and advertising.

Management: Supervise, delegate responsibility, train employees, evaluate others, motivate employees, manage budgets and finances, resolve crises, identify breaches in ethics, and deal with multicultural issues.

Assess and Diagnose: Attend to visual detail, diagnose, test, evaluate, and administer tests.

Repair: Repair equipment, maintain, install, inspect, and monitor.

Administration and Clerical: Manage time, coordinate events, arrange meetings, schedule appointments, organize time and duties, prioritize multiple projects, and use computer applications and office equipment.

People: Manage, schedule, teach, train, resolve disputes, mediate differences, advise, counsel, guide, treat, help, and assist.

Identifying Your Skills Exercise

Write down all your previous positions. Then, list your primary job duties. Next, list the skills and abilities that were necessary to accomplish each task. Do not limit yourself to full-time jobs. Also include part-time work, volunteer positions, and work on community projects or committees. Perhaps you served as the president of your local homeowners' association, thereby developing leadership skills, negotiation abilities, and knowledge of budgeting processes. After doing this exercise, you will probably uncover a number of talents you had not considered.

Education: _____

Current Job Title: _____
    Job Duties: _____
    Specific Skills: _____

Previous Job Title: _____
    Job Duties: _____
    Specific Skills: _____

Previous Job Title: _____
    Job Duties: _____
    Specific Skills: _____

Employers want to know what you have *done*, and the way to convey that information is by highlighting results and accomplishments, not just by listing the job duties you performed. To help you identify accomplishments, think about the following situations and write down examples from your past work:

- Solved a customer's problem that lead to customer satisfaction
- Came up with an idea that saved time, made money, or saved money
- Helped your team create a marketing campaign or a new product
- Developed a new course, brochure, training video, or the like
- Identified a new marketing niche
- Streamlined a procedure
- Served a client
- Helped a customer resolve a problem

Transferable personal characteristics that are also relevant include cooperation, organization, vision, leadership, the ability to see the big picture, and being results-oriented, dependable, and ethical.

THE 30-SECOND MARKETING PITCH

The 30-second advertisement, or "elevator pitch," as it's commonly referred to, is a short, comprehensive, opening statement that presents a job seeker's qualifications to a potential employer. This self-advertisement is often used in situations like career fairs when there is a limited time to speak to a potential employer.

When developing your self-marketing script, be brief, specific, and emphasize your accomplishments. Keep your script no more than two minutes long. Present your most important points first. Focus on your best traits that relate to the position. Then provide a concise summary your knowledge, skills, experience, and most relevant accomplishments. Highlight relevant experience to the position but save the details for later. Then mention any additional qualities such as dedication, enthusiasm, creativity, or organization.

Examples

Consider the following examples of the 30-second self-marketing pitch:

I've spent the past ten years as a marketing director for a mid-sized credit union, where I wrote numerous press releases, created training brochures, and edited a newsletter that was distributed to over 3,500 members. Two years ago, I decided to pursue my real passion in journalism by finishing my degree in journalism and am now looking for a position as an editor with a publishing company (such as yours).

I recently completed a master's degree in counseling. I have over 10 years of experience in higher education from previous positions in admissions and financial aid and five years of academic advising and career counseling at Northern University before deciding to focus on personal counseling. While at Northern I developed a series of brown bag group sessions for students featuring a variety of common college stressors such as college adjustment issues, relationship issues, stress management, and self-esteem issues. I hope to bring my counseling skills to the community sector.

I am a conceptually creative individual who is fluent in both Spanish and English. When my company decided to downsize, I took the opportunity to go back to school to pursue a longstanding interest in graphic design. Among some of the projects I have completed are a series of new product marketing promotions for a retail fashion line and several Web sites for local businesses in our area.

Practice until you know the key points well, but do not try to memorize your self-marketing pitch word for word. You want to sound confident, but not dry and rehearsed. Use your 30-second marketing pitch when talking to recruiters at job fairs or making initial networking contacts, for profession branding statements on social networking sites, in the summary section of your resume and in your cover letter, when making job inquiries, and when applying for a job in person or in an interview situation.

Using Skills in a Resume

In a resume, skills are usually denoted as verbs that show some kind of action as performed, not just a list of job duties. For example, "answered phones" is a job duty but does not really address the skill involved in performing that job duty. Ask yourself, Who did I talk to? What was the purpose of the call? What was the result of the call? Did I resolve a problem, answer a question, or provide information? In answering such questions, you may discover that you did something like "helped customers" or "resolved problems with orders," which can then be written as "helped customers successfully complete the ordering process" or "resolved customer's complaints in a timely manner." Now your "answered phones" (job duty) has been more effectively translated into the skill you performed, "resolved customer's complaints."

When applying for jobs, the trick is to match your skill set as closely as possible to the skills required for a position. Hiring managers are really only interested in a small number of essential skills for the position they are advertising. Based on what they read in your resume, they will determine whether or not you deserve to be invited in for an interview. Many people make the mistake of listing job duties. Do not assume an employer can automatically decipher your skill set. Instead, make your skills very clear to a potential employer by spelling them out in your cover letter, on your resume, and during the interview.

Now you are ready to summarize those skills for the *Summary* section of your resume.

Example of a Skills-based Summary Section of a Resume

- *Over 12 years' experience in a human resources environment.*
- *13 years' customer service interfacing with the public.*
- *Strong interpersonal skills, able to develop effective working relationships with people from a wide variety of backgrounds.*
- *Able to maintain confidentiality and exercise sound, independent judgment.*

Here are some more examples of skill-based responsibilities to include in summaries for a variety of positions.

Examples of Human Resources Skills

- Extensive experience with SAP software timekeeping for 80+ employees.
- Maintained accuracy of payroll for 30 officers.
- Trained and oriented new employees and developed a New Employee Handbook.
- Monitored and enforced compliance with all OSHA regulations.

Examples of Computer Skills

- Identifies and resolves critical path and network logic conflicts.
- Strong working knowledge of Microsoft Works, Excel, Outlook Power Point, and Access.
- Programming proficiency in Visual Basic, C++, and Oracle applications.
- Responsible for software configuration, application run-time configuration, capacity planning, and first-level problem support.

Examples of Management Skills

- Led nine-member team of engineering, production, quality, production management, and vendor personnel to improve repair times and reduce costs for technical systems overhaul.
- Solid interpersonal, motivational, and presentation skills backed by hands-on, assertive management style and experience directing global, cross-functional teams.
- Supervised a team of 20 programmers and 3 business analysts.
- Managed all phases of opening and operating the first four McDonald's restaurants in the state of Vermont.

Examples of Writing and Editing Skills

- Authored and updated content for a regional Web page.
- Wrote and edited articles from Wildlife Conservation officers to be published in *Game News.*
- Updated and edited descriptions for new furniture designs, assisted in photo shoots, updated information on new furniture designs.
- Created advertising copy for new products on Web site.

Examples of Customer Service Skills

- Relayed information to public regarding hunting regulations and policies.
- Developed strong interpersonal relationships with employees and central office personnel.
- Diplomatically resolved customer complaints.
- Effectively developed telephone communication.

Examples of Office Skills

- Computerized and improved many existing antiquated systems, methods, and processes.
- Administered memberships for the Recreation Center.
- Provided back-up support for Accounts Receivables Department as needed.
- Operated multiline phone system, scheduled appointments, and made travel arrangements for staff.

Examples of Organizational Skills

- Organized summer programs in Adult Education Department at Kings College.
- Conducted meetings and presided over a booster club.
- Able to prioritize projects and meet deadlines in a fast-paced advertising agency.
- Organized community outreach programs for a nonprofit Alzheimer's support organization.
- Coordinated volunteers and student activities for the Ross Elementary Parent-Teacher Organization.

Examples of Sales and Marketing Skills

- Sold long-distance telecommunications services for the third-largest residential long-distance career service in Northeastern Pennsylvania.
- Developed promotional brochures for new product promotion campaign.
- Maintained a successful track record of establishing key referral accounts and increasing market share.

Examples of Broadcast Communications Skills

- Wrote and produced public service announcements.
- Organized news releases for local newspaper, radio, TV, and client customer base.
- Oversaw production of news team serving a midsized radio market.
- Arranged for publicity and feature stories with local media.

Examples of Health Care Skills

- Responsible for the care of elderly people to include bathing, feeding, dressing, changing, positioning, and relaying complaints and information from the client to the nurse.
- Provided routine respiratory care, patient evaluation, and assessment.
- Provided comprehensive diagnostic and treatment services for speech- and language-disordered children and adults.

- Involved in treatment planning and implementation.
- Maintained progress notes and generated assessment and treatment reports.

Examples of Teaching and Training Skills

- Developed lesson plans for preschool children.
- Team taught PA Science courses at the secondary school level.
- Provided training to end-users in conjunction with the College's instructional technologist.
- Ten years of experience teaching ESL students in a public school setting.

Examples of Technical Skills

- Performed calibration, repair, maintenance, and circuit analysis on diagnostic equipment.
- Developed guidelines for laboratory's new quality control procedures.
- Implemented Total Quality Management procedures in a paper products—manufacturing facility.
- Built electrical test equipment for customer service and in-house testing, motor testing, circuit board repair, and PLC repair.

Chapter 5

THE BENEFITS OF YOUR
AGE AND EXPERIENCE

Age and experience will beat youth and enthusiasm every time.

Anonymous

THE REALITIES OF AGE DISCRIMINATION

According to a 2007 AARP study, 60 percent of respondents believe age discrimination exists in the workplace and 13 percent have personally experienced such discrimination in the past five years. A July 2005 job application experiment found that candidates over 50 had to submit more applications to receive an interview. Specifically, candidates under age 50 were 40 percent more likely to be called for an interview than those older than 50.[1] Furthermore, 77 percent of workers "actually have experienced or observed" workplace age bias, and 78 percent report that age bias is a "fact of life."[2]

A LITTLE GOOD NEWS

Despite the realities of age discrimination, there are employers who value the experience of older workers. As our society becomes more accustomed to older workers in the workplace, ageism will decrease. When searching for a job in your new career field, there are ways you can minimize the concerns some employers have about hiring older employees while emphasizing the advantages of your age. The key is to be able to discern whether your inability to find a job is because of age bias or because of factors within your control. If your lack of success in the job market is a result of factors you can control, then you have a greater range of options available to improve your situation. These options may be as simple as updating your wardrobe, coloring your hair, answering interview questions differently, or modifying body language.

Unless you were involved in the hiring process in a previous position or have become "interview savvy" through multiple experiences, you will, like most people, really have no idea of how you come off compared with other candidates. You also do not know who your competition is. The other candidate may be fresh out of college or someone with equal qualifications, or he or she may be someone with many years of experience.

When considering which new career field to enter, be careful not to make career decisions based on hearsay without checking out the facts firsthand. Not all employers consider age as a negative. The key is to find those employers who value the experience and maturity an older worker will provide over the long run versus the short-term savings in hiring an inexperienced graduate. Many employers are now seeking older workers for the expertise and wisdom they bring to the workplace. Still others view mature employees as mentors who may provide knowledge transfer to younger staff.

The other piece of good news is that there should be plenty of opportunities for workers of all ages in the coming years. One of the greatest challenges facing corporate leaders over the next decade is the pending explosion in the number of workers reaching retirement age and the inadequate pool of younger workers to fill those roles. The loss of experienced workers when they retire will create a gaping knowledge void. At the college where I work, we have experienced a number of retirements of senior staff people in such key areas of the college as registration and admissions. The loss of the retirees' 30 years of experience and knowledge will be felt for some time, despite attempts to train the retirees' replacements. Some companies view retirements as a cost-saving effort, but this is very short-sighted considering the loss of knowledge, experience, and intangible work values of loyalty, commitment, and quality. Such employers are also not taking into account the negative effects of burnout and resentment an increased workload will have on those employees who are forced to pick up the retiree's share of the workload.

Many companies have started planning for the transition by beefing up their recruiting efforts and restructuring positions to retain older workers through phased retirement, flex time, and part-time options. Hopefully, more companies will follow suit and offer more attractive opportunities to retain older workers.

COMMON MYTHS ABOUT OLDER WORKERS

Employers may buy the stereotype that older workers are out-of-date; cannot use technology; are rigid, opinionated, and in poor health; and will not work very long anyway.[3] The facts are that older workers tend to take less sick days than their younger counterparts, are less accident-prone, are more productive, have the experience to handle unusual situations, have a better work ethic, and have a stronger sense of responsibility, ownership, and loyalty to the company. I've spoken with several human resource managers who say that an older worker's experience and track record of success and reliability is something that's missing in the Millennial generation. Regarding the stereotype of rigidness, consider that some older workers may be more willing to share their opinion than others, but there are plenty of workers in their twenties who are just as stubborn, opinionated, and unwilling to embrace change.

In many ways, employers are getting more "bang for their buck" by hiring an experienced employee as compared with a younger or more inexperienced worker who will require more training or on-the-job experience. Older workers are used to hard work and generally do a better job than their younger counterparts because they actually *want* to be at work.

Another major myth about older workers is that they are harder to train and cannot learn things as quickly as younger workers. We have all heard older people lament, "I can't be bothered with all those new gadgets" or "I'll never figure out how to use my computer." This scenario is based on a few individuals and stems more from individual fear, lack of motivation, and a self-fulfilling prophecy than an accurate description of the abilities of people over 50. While the younger generation does have the advantage of having grown up using computers, cell phones, and the Internet, I know of many older people who can use the computer or their cell phone as well as any 20-year-old. Look at the growing number of Baby Boomers using Facebook.

While it is true that that older workers may require additional time to learn new material, they are capable of learning, and learning well, for evidence indicates they have greater retention, show higher learning achievement, and are far more likely to complete a new field of study than are their younger counterparts.[4] Such abilities put midlife career changers in a perfect position. Having just revived education or training to upgrade skills or acquire a new degree definitively disproves the notion that you are too old to learn new things.

BENEFITS OF OLDER WORKERS

Let's look at what you can bring to the table. In general, older adults have larger vocabularies, command a greater understanding of written material, contain more ability to reason, and display good judgment based on experience than do younger people.

According to a 2009 National Association of Colleges and Employers (NACE) survey, employers reported that students lacked a good work ethic.[5] Specifically, students had trouble with time management and were unable to multi-task to meet deadlines. This is where experienced workers and those of the Baby Boomer generation can really shine. Because older workers have been in the workforce for many years, they can emphasize traits that younger, less experienced workers do not possess: loyalty to organizational goals; commitment to quality customer service; record of reliability and responsibility. and level of patience and wisdom that comes from years of experience. If you are an older worker who has been a manager, think of what you have observed and learned over the course of your career. You have seen bosses come and go and have watched companies struggle to remain competitive, make costly mistakes, create strategic plans, and enact company policies that were eventually replaced with other policies. You have seen what works and what does not work, and that information is priceless.

According to a survey of human resources managers, these are the top qualities of older employees:

1. Loyalty and dedication to the company
2. Commitment to doing quality work
3. Reliability in a crisis
4. Solid performance record
5. Basic skills in reading, writing, and arithmetic

6. Solid experience in job and/or industry
7. Camaraderie with coworkers[6]

Not surprisingly, the qualities identified by human resources managers are also ones that employers most desire in employees.

Other benefits that older workers bring to the workplace include the following characteristics:

- *Punctuality.* Older workers look forward to going to work each day, so they are likely to arrive on time, thus preventing gaps in coverage. Their children are usually grown, so they do not need to leave to stay home with a sick child (although they may need to leave to take care of a sick parent or grandchild).
- *Honesty.* Honesty is a common value among older workers whose values include personal integrity and a desire for the truth.
- *Attentiveness.* Older employees listen well. They have the experience to supplement their experience and know what needs to be done without having to be told twice.
- *Maturity.* Having years of life and work experiences makes older workers less susceptible to stress and leaves them less rattled when problems do occur. Older workers are often able to transfer their knowledge and life lessons to other workers and thus often serve as mentors to younger employees.
- *Customer focus.* Older workers have been schooled in old-fashioned customer service, proper telephone etiquette, manners, and common sense. These traits are priceless! Older workers recognize the importance of customer service and can relate to clients in a more professional and mature manner.
- *Work ethic.* Older workers are not averse to doing what needs to be done to complete the project or report and to do it well. Working hard, doing their best, coming to work on time and not leaving early, taking on responsibility, and not calling in sick unless they are really sick are some of the examples of the type of work ethic older workers share. Baby Boomers were raised on the mantra "If it's not done well, it's not worth doing." These are invaluable traits in a time where employers are complaining about lack of soft employee skills in younger workers.
- *Common courtesies.* Courtesies are nothing more than good manners. For example: telling the boss in advance about vacation plans or notifying the boss if you are going to be late for a meeting; treating customers and fellow workers with respect; recognizing corporate structure and respecting hierarchy. Many older workers are well versed in the old-school office and managerial procedures of answering the telephone, greeting customers, relating to superiors, typing correspondence, conducting a meeting, writing a report, wearing appropriate work dress, and using professional language. Some of these factors reflect generational differences. Baby Boomers did not grow up texting their friends and do not consider piercings and flip-flops as appropriate office attire.

Your job is to dispel the employer's assumptions about older workers. Here are some ways to do that:

- Project an energetic, professional, and competent image. Assure an employer that you are fully qualified to do the job (mentally, physically, and psychologically) by the way you interact, dress, and speak.
- Dress professionally and appropriately for your age without wearing clothes or a hairstyle that is out-of-date.
- Highlight recent accomplishments or provide examples by means of a physical or electronic portfolio containing samples of your best work.
- Keep up-to-date with technology. Show younger hiring managers that you are up to speed with using a computer, e-mail, mobile technology, and the Internet. If you are applying for a sales position, highlight your ability to use smart phones, a laptop, or Web 2.0 technology. If you are applying for an office or marketing position, show that you know the latest Microsoft Office applications, how to post a blog, or how to connect with professionals through a social networking site such as LinkedIn.
- Convey a positive, enthusiastic, and cooperative attitude. Do not complain about your past employer, bemoan your children, or rant about your pet peeves. While it's okay to state an opinion if asked, you also need to appear flexible and open to new ideas. And above all else, convey enthusiasm about your potential new job, even if you have seen it all before and can do it in your sleep.
- Treat whoever you interview with, whether younger or older than you, as a contemporary. Resist the tendency to give a "history lesson" or "talk down" to interviewers younger than you. You'll meet less resistance if you treat everyone in a friendly and collegial manner.
- Keep the discussion focused on your relevant professional skills and knowledge. Do not spend valuable interview time telling "war" stories, showing off your knowledge, sharing too many details of your personal life, or commiserating about current events. Give brief, relevant, and concrete answers to interview questions using examples to illustrate how your experience can help a potential employer.
- Realize that the interview is about how you can help the employer, not how they can help you. The more you understand your prospective employer's current situation and issues, the better you can match your experience and skills to the employer's needs in a way that will make you the logical choice to hire.

Step back to take an honest look at yourself as others would perceive you. Then, update your computer skills, your job search and interviewing techniques, your attitude, and your appearance as needed. As the television ad goes, you want to "look like you know what you're doing *and* can still do it!"

Choose Your Job Openings Carefully

You have a better chance applying for jobs in markets that are not age-conscious or in industries where experience matters. Each autumn, AARP puts out a list of age-friendly employers at "Best Employers for Workers Over 50" at http://www.aarp.org.

Such industries as health care, sales, marketing, education, and management, as well as the field of consulting, are more "elder-friendly" and recognize the value of life experience. Whether or not older workers can successfully land another position is dependent upon several factors: their skill set, how current they are in their field or with technology, how they present themselves in an interview, the particular needs of the employer, and the employer's attitudes on aging.

If your career change plan includes going back to school for professional training, you will have no experience in your new field even though you may have lots of life experience and maturity. If you are applying for a trainee position, then the company to which you are applying will more likely to want someone who does not have well-developed opinions and prejudices—in other words, someone the company can shape. In this case, you may be better off applying for the position of training the new trainees (which would utilize and value your experience and wisdom). So it will pay to choose your job openings carefully. Search for job postings that use words like "maturity," "good judgment," "career-minded," and "work experience."

Another tactic is to target smaller companies or companies that are just starting up. Smaller companies will value an employee that has the flexibility to handle unrelated tasks, and new companies can use your expertise and experience. Realize that smaller companies may not be able to pay as much as larger companies.

Despite the realities of age discrimination and the difficulty of finding jobs in tough economic times, it is possible to find employment. The key is to sell yourself effectively, search for openings and network aggressively, interview well, and be willing to be flexible.

Chapter 6

UNDERSTAND
WHO YOU ARE

I believe we are given two lives: the one we learn with and the one we live after.
Glenn Close in *Dangerous Liaisons*

There is something about growing older (and, one hopes, wiser) that compels us to take a step back to ponder the meaning of our lives. Time begins to feel shorter and more valuable. According to Carl Jung, meaning and purpose become important in midlife. This is often the time people begin to reevaluate their lives and reexamine their values and priorities. They ask themselves if the career they are currently holding is really what they want to continue to do, or is there something else they would like to pursue. Is the lifestyle they're leading one that they want to continue? And if it is not, then how do they want to spend the remaining years of their lives? For people who are very achievement oriented and tend to define themselves by their job title, it may be difficult to separate their personal self and desires from their professional image. Figuring out what to do next will require some serious soul-searching and listening to what you truly want to do versus what you think you should be doing. In other words, finding the real *you*.

WHY DO YOU WORK?

People work for a variety of reasons besides the obvious reason of being able to pay the bills and put food on the table. According to a recent Bankrate survey, employed Americans cited their paycheck as the top reason they are staying in their job (39 percent).[1] But enjoyment of their work came in a close second (33 percent). Surprisingly, health insurance was a distant third (11 percent). Seven percent said their main reason for working is having a good boss. When asked what they would do if they were to win the lottery or come into enough money that they did not have to work anymore, most people said that they would prefer to bank the money and continue working. Fifty percent opted to keep their job, compared to 14 percent who would turn in their two weeks' notice right away, 13 percent who would start their own business, and 17 percent who said they would take time off to decide.

Exercise 1: Why Are You Working?

Check all the reasons that apply to you.

___ Earn a living
___ Receive benefits (health, tuition reimbursement, company car, etc.)
___ Gain expertise, respect, power, prestige, status
___ Enjoyment (enjoy tasks at least 75 percent of the time)
___ Intellectual stimulation
___ Provides structure to the day, gives you something to do
___ Accomplishment of doing something well
___ Relationships, sense of connection
___ Pursue a passion
___ A sense of meaning
___ A way to give back to others, make a difference, do good works

You have probably discovered that there is more than one reason why you work, and you may have noticed your reasons for working have changed over the years. What was important in your twenties may not be as important in your forties or fifties.

WORK AND LIFE BALANCE

Many professional people in midlife wrestle with the issue of maintaining a successful career that also allows for family and personal time.

Balancing work and life becomes an important issue for people in midlife. Every day, people struggle to meet the demands of their jobs, children, school, parents, social life, community responsibilities, and financial matters. Finding a work-life balance is especially difficult for people who have spent enormous time and poured energy into building a high-profile career at the expense of their personal lives. Twelve-hour work days and a constant connection to the office through BlackBerries, laptops, and cell phones are not conducive to creating an appropriate work-life balance.

In their book *Midlife Crisis at 30*, authors Lia Macko and Kerry Rubin point out that the major milestones in a Baby Boomer woman's life (marriage, motherhood, and career) have been stretched out over the course of a lifetime.[2] Today's young women, typically in their thirties, are experiencing the rise of their careers at the same time that they are getting married and having children—right around their 30th birthdays. As a result, high-achieving young women, who want to be as successful in their personal lives as they are in their professional ones, are experiencing overload. This situation has lead to what the authors call the new "midlife crisis at 30."

Humans were never meant to be one-dimensional beings. They have psychological, social, physical, mental, creative, and spiritual needs. Individuals who are emotionally balanced are generally happier and are better able to meet and deal with the demands of life that come from good events like job promotions, marriage, and children as well as such unexpected events as illness, job stress, divorce, or death of family members. Lack of balance can leave a person feeling out of sync, fatigued, and depressed and can create a whole host of other complications arising from not eating properly or not getting enough sleep to relying on drugs, alcohol, and other forms of self-medication.

Many people think they have to spend time in the beginning stages of their career devoting themselves fully to their jobs in order to advance and succeed. In fact, many industries encourage that type of work culture. There is nothing wrong with dedicating yourself to your career or taking pride in your job title as long as you have a network of relationships, hobbies, or other activities outside of work to provide stress relief and spiritual renewal. However, if you are spending all your week and your weekends at the office, or if work is the last thing you think about before you fall asleep at night and the first thing on your mind when you wake up in the morning, then you are heading for an emotional and physical collapse.

The challenge we individuals each face is to develop our own methods for balancing the demands of work and personal life according to our personal values. Some people can establish balance by setting boundaries to protect their personal life by not taking business calls after 8:00 at night or by only checking their e-mail once a day on weekends. Other people will decide to "step out" of their career for a while to raise a family or start their own business; yet others will choose to find a different boss or switch to a career or an industry that does not demand that they blur the lines between their personal and professional lives. In their quest to resolve the balance issue, some people may have to redefine their personal definition of success by replacing "having it all" with "having enough."

Sharon

Sharon was a 44-year-old married woman with a 14-year-old son and a 12-year-old daughter.

I was doing very well as a travel agent until the market changed after 9/11. Now everyone books their flights online. Then I had a chance to do some advertising work with a local visitor's bureau, which really got me interested in the graphic design—web page advertising business. Today, my husband and I are partners in an advertising business. Now that my kids are getting older, I'm looking for something a little more stable. The ad life is getting too hectic and you are constantly needing to keep up with the technology or be left behind.

Sharon was looking for a way to balance her work and the demands of a growing family. She did not want a fast-paced, hectic lifestyle anymore. Sharon has always been interested in health and fitness and thought that she would like to work with children in promoting healthy eating habits. After exploring her options, she decided to enroll in a bachelor's program in dietetics at a local university. Because she's potentially looking at three and a half to four years to complete her degree, she decided to enroll full-time to complete her degree as quickly as possible and to be eligible for the maximum amount of financial aid available.

Sharon owns her own business, so she can work around her classes and hopes to be finished with school by the time her son graduates from high school.

CAREER DEVELOPMENT ACROSS THE LIFE SPAN

Career development, in my opinion, is ultimately about figuring out who you are and finding your place in the work world. I often hear adults say, "I always wanted to be a teacher [fill in the blank with your own dream career]" or "When I was in high school, I wanted to go into fashion design." Many of us had a general idea of what we wanted to be when we grew up. Then we graduated from high school, went to college, and drifted in and out of a state of indecision before finally majoring in *something*.

I remember living on a college dorm floor with a very artistically gifted young woman who was majoring in pre-med. She came from a family of physicians and was expected to follow in the same career path. Although I do not remember her name, what sticks in my mind is that what she really wanted to do was major in painting but her family expected her to become a physician. I do not know if she ever became a physician, but if she did I bet she ended up doing a career change sometime during her life. The point of the story is that many people graduate from college in a major that may have been the best option for them at the time. Later, after spending a few years working, they discover what they really want to do. Personal career development occurs for each of us at our own time. Sometimes it's just a matter of developing into the person you were meant to be.

Previous models of career development have suggested that our career development progresses along a linear career path that begins in our twenties, peaks in midlife, and slowly phases out to end in retirement. Unfortunately, that scenario is no longer valid in today's rapidly changing world. Today, careers are marked by interruptions and are continued in new, and often unforeseen, directions. There is no longer a stigma attached to changing careers or jobs as there was in the past. Today's career journeys are all about creating better opportunities for the future.

Viewing career development across the life span from a holistic perspective, some career experts are now using the term *career life* to acknowledge the multiple roles that people hold today that lead to satisfying, purposeful, and meaningful lives.[3] A woman who has a career as a physician may also be a wife and mother, a volunteer at the local genealogical society, a caretaker to her aging parents, choir director at church, and a golfer and tennis player in her leisure hours. All these activities add value and provide meaning to the nonwork aspects of her life—to her personal, social, and spiritual life—and serve to enrich and balance her career life. The emergence of terms such as *career life* reflects a sensitivity to the numerous challenges facing most people as they struggle to balance multiple life roles.

In our current turbulent economic times, in which people are dealing with shifting job markets, possible downsizing, and job loss, traditional career development theories are no longer adequate to describe modern career development. The concept of an absolute, one-time career choice is being replaced by new concepts that include career adaptability, mastery of different roles, and short-term decision making.[4] These modern theories contain an appreciation for the normalcy of dealing with career starts, delays, detours, and stops in our career development. Today, our challenge is to find a new, economically and personally satisfying way to exist in a changing work environment.

Planned happenstance,[5] a career development theory, is a belief that one should expect the unexpected and capitalize on unplanned events to turn them into career opportunities. This can mean anything from viewing a layoff as an opportunity to leave a job you hate and go back to school or accepting an internship with a company you never heard of before that then leads to a job after graduation.

Some writers have suggested that as life expectancy increases, changes in middle age may become an "existential necessity."[6] This means that psychologically, as well as economically, we may need to change careers. Some of these midlife changes will be internally driven. Professionals may feel that their work is no longer satisfying and that they want new challenges, or they may decide that it's time to pursue a long-forgotten hobby or talent. Other midlife changes will be triggered by such external events as a company closure or unemployment.

CAREER DECISION MAKING

Career researchers have studied people's job decision-making strategies. What they found was that people who relied on both rational decision-making and intuitive thinking styles (thinking with their "gut") reported a higher awareness of themselves and their work environment, which helped them make a better career choice.[7] Despite the popular myth, career paths are not linear, and there is no right or perfect job or career for anyone (believe me, I've tried). In reality, there are a number of career options that may be right for you, and there are many roads that can lead to the same career destination.

If you know you want to do something else but are not sure what it is, one place to start is by taking an interest inventory. Among the most popular standardized instruments are the *Strong Interest Inventory*, the *Self-Directed Search*, and the *Myers-Briggs Type Indicator.* Standardized career assessments are available through your local college or university and through private life or career coaches or professional counselors. Career assessments will not tell you what you should be—they will not, for example, tell you that you "should be a medical technician"—but they will provide you with a list of career possibilities that match your interests, values, and personality type. To get the most out of the process, you should review the results with a trained career professional who can translate your results into concrete career options.

Abilities do play a role in the types of careers a person can be successful in. Adults usually have a better gauge of where their true strengths lie by virtue of life and work experience. We are all blessed with natural talents and abilities, but some people may not realize the extent of their abilities because of social conditioning, gender, or ethnic stereotyping; experiences in school; and the messages they received from parents, teachers, and other well-intentioned individuals. Think about such statements as "Women are not suited for careers in engineering or medicine" or "Men don't become nurses" and how much times have changed.

Self-concept has a lot to do with the careers we consider or ignore. A positive or negative self-concept acts as a filter that can expand or limit our choices. Think about the messages you have heard over the years and the ones you still tell yourself. When I was an academic advisor, the college I worked for calculated that students who wanted to avoid any major that involved math had automatically ruled out about 51 percent of the majors offered at that college. Realistically evaluate your strengths, weaknesses, skills, attitudes, and interests, and create your own definition of who you are and what you can or cannot do.

GET THE FACTS

There are literally thousands of occupations available in the workplace. Most of us have never even heard of half of them unless we've been exposed to them in school, have seen them portrayed on television, or personally know of a friend or neighbor who is in that field. I know of several individuals who did not "discover" their career passion, especially fields considered nontraditional to gender careers, until they were exposed to them during college or until someone said, "Hey, have you ever thought about going into . . . ?"

With all the occupations to choose from today, how do you find one that will lead to a satisfying and productive career? The answer is by doing your research. Occupational research is critical to making a good career choice because it is the key to uncovering possible career options and correcting any faulty beliefs you might have picked up along the way. Finding out what a person in a particular occupation actually does in his or her job will help you make a better, more informed career decision. In real life, occupations are not always as glamorous as they're portrayed on television or in books. Doing your research before you make your career move is critical to determining whether the new career will pay enough to support you and your family and be satisfying enough to make the demands of additional schooling or credentialing worth the effort and investment of time and money. Research can be done by talking with people who are in an occupation that you are considering, reading about occupations in books at your local library, or researching them on the Internet. A simple way to research careers on the Internet is to do a Google search. Simply type "careers in nutrition" (or whatever career or occupation you are interested in) in the search box, and hundreds of links will appear beginning with the hits that are the most popular or relevant. When doing your research, try to find out what a person in your chosen job or profession does during the day, how much the job pays a year, what education or credentials are needed, and what the future job growth is expected to be for that profession. Also try to learn the best ways to land a job in your new field.

Identify several career options that contain what you enjoy doing, allow you to use your skills and talents, and will help you obtain what is important to you. If you are having difficulty deciding between several strong interests, try to make a distinction between what you want to do to earn a living and what you want to pursue as a hobby.

Get the facts before you rule out any options, and be aware of biases based on incomplete or faulty information about careers (for example, teachers do not make very much money or retail jobs are about folding sweaters at the GAP). Research can only take you so far. Eventually, you will need to directly experience your new career. If you are interested in becoming a physical therapist, for instance, call your local rehab center to see if there are therapists who would spend a few minutes talking to you about what they like and do not like about their job and how they got into their career. Ask if they will let you experience the job firsthand by following them around for a morning (also called *job shadowing*).

Start taking classes if you need to retrain, or begin looking for job openings if you need to search for a new job. Once you have begun working toward your new career, you'll be able to reflect on and review your decision at various intervals. People make adjustments in their career paths all the time, and there is nothing wrong with that. It's all just part of the career transition process.

SELF-REFLECTIVE EXERCISES

For those of you who would benefit from learning to listen to yourself at a deeper level, the following exercises can help you begin to unlock your inner dreams and desires. However, if you already have a clear idea of what you want to change your career to, then you can skip the rest of this chapter and proceed to Chapter 8, "Careers to Consider."

Exercise 2: Career Timeline

Spend some time looking back over the course of events that led you to the career or job you are in today. Draw a timeline beginning with your first job in high school and including every job you have held since then. Identify why you applied for those positions. Did you grab the first job you found after high school or college? Did a friend or family member suggest you study a certain major? Were you expected to follow a parent's footsteps or contribute to the family business? Highlight the jobs you enjoyed to see if there are any patterns. When you look over your timeline, what do you learn about yourself and your work life? How can you use this information to make a more satisfying career plan for the future?

Exercise 3: Identifying Your "Shoulds"

Some people are so trapped by their "shoulds," or sense of responsibility, that it may be difficult for them to access their true inner desires. One adult learner in her forties described the process this way: "This time I'm looking inside. Instead of listening to what everyone else says I should do, I'm looking at what *I* want to do for a change."

Write down your "shoulds" on a piece of paper, and then throw the list away. Make a new list without the "shoulds."

Exercise 4: Who Am I?

Try to be spontaneous when answering the following questions, and do not censor your answers.

1. I am _____
2. I need _____
3. I wish _____
4. I am motivated by _____
5. I am satisfied with _____
6. I would like to change _____
7. I am at my best when _____
8. I am not at my best when _____
9. I often feel _____
10. I rarely feel _____

Exercise 5: People, Data, Things

Identifying career interests in terms of people, data, or things is a commonly used career exploration exercise that can quickly help you identify potentially satisfying careers. Begin by answering this question: Which would you prefer to work with on a daily basis, **People, Data, Things**? Circle your answer.

If you have chosen People, explore careers that help others or provide a service to others. Consider the careers in the following areas:

- Teaching
- Counseling and Social Services
- Medicine and Health Care
- Fitness and Nutrition
- Personal Services
- Sales
- Customer Service
- Management
- Legal Services
- Entertainment

If you have chosen Data, consider careers that involve facts, numbers, or business procedures. Look for careers in the following areas:

- Accounting
- Computer Programming or IT
- Mathematics
- Office Procedures
- Writing
- Research

If you have chosen Things, look at areas of work that involve building and making things; working outdoors; or working with animals, plants, wood, metals, or technology. Explore the following careers:

- Heavy Equipment Operator
- Landscaper
- Carpenter
- Cook
- Craftsperson
- Animal Trainer or Technician
- Horticulturist
- Artist
- Auto Mechanic

Exercise 6: Career Goal Sentence Exercise
Read the following sentence and fill in the blanks.

(Do What?)   (To Whom or What?)

(Type of Industry)   *(Person, Thing, Data, Animal)*

I want to _____**(teach)**_____**(children)**_____.

(Under what conditions?)   (Where?)

(Job Skill)   *(Physical Location*

about/who are____**(autistic)**_____ **in a** ____**(Public School)**_____.

(Why?)

(Value)

because___**(I can make a difference in their lives)** _____.

Chapter 7

CAREER CHANGE OPTIONS

Freedom is knowing your options.

Helen Harkness

When you are considering a second career, there are several factors to keep in mind:

- What is the level of skill, education, or specialized training needed to perform the job?
- Do the elements of this career match my interests, abilities, and values?
- Does the career or occupation provide a direct or necessary service or product, or can the work be outsourced?
- Will this career be dramatically affected by shifts in the economy?
- Will the demand for the career still be there in the next 10 or 20 years?
- Does the career provide upward mobility or the opportunity to acquire new skills through education?

FUTURE CAREER TRENDS

According to the Bureau of Labor Statistics (BLS) projections to 2018, the two industry sectors expected to have the largest employment growth are professional and business services, and healthcare and social assistance.[1] The goods-producing sector is expected to show virtually no growth. The registered nursing occupation is projected to add the most new jobs followed by home health aides and customer service representatives.[2] The top three fastest growing occupations are expected to be biomedical engineers, network systems and data communications analysts, and home health aides.[3] For the latest projections and a list of the fastest-growing occupations see www.bls.gov/emp or www.bls.gov/mir.

Currently, there are nationwide worker shortages in engineering and science. At the college level, there are faculty shortages in science, engineering, nursing, and such allied health care programs as physical therapy, radiologic science, and medical laboratory sciences.[4] Because of the number of Baby Boomers who will soon be retiring (almost 40 percent of the labor force), worker shortages are predicted in education, government, utilities, the oil and gas industry, chemical companies, and the aerospace industry.

In many parts of the country, utility companies and state and federal agencies are ramping up recruiting efforts on college campuses in preparation for openings that will be left by retiring Baby Boomers. Civil service positions within state or federal government are often overlooked career options. But as corporations continue to get leaner and nonprofits are increasingly strapped for cash, the government is becoming an employer of choice. Government positions offer excellent job security, good pay, ample sick days, holidays, vacation days, and outstanding health and retirement benefits. Although the application process can be a bit daunting, the wait is well worth the effort.

SECOND-CAREER ALTERNATIVES

Teaching is a popular second-career choice because it offers rewarding work, provides a competitive salary, and is relatively immune to economic fluctuations. Employment of schoolteachers will continue to grow during 2008-2018 as a result of new job openings and retirements, according to the Bureau of Labor Statistics.[5] Many colleges and universities now offer part-time teacher certification programs, accelerated programs, and the option of earning your teaching degree online.

The health care field is also a good second-career choice for career changers of all ages. The variety of job opportunities, the diverse settings, and the promise of good salaries make health care careers an attractive option. Many people are turning to health care as a way to provide purpose through caring for others. Nursing homes, hospices, and assisted living centers will continue to grow, as will home health care. These careers offer great benefits as well as flexible hours.

Career changers who have science or math backgrounds and have worked in private industry can easily make a career transition to education or sales, or they can become valuable consultants to companies in related industries, city government, or nonprofit or other grass-roots organizations. They can also find employment as editors or science consultants to book and trade magazine publishers.

Individuals with an analytical ability along with a statistics background may want to consider upgrading their skills in human subjects research to qualify for institutional research positions at colleges and universities.

If you have a knack for sales or customer service, you can apply those skills to develop a second career with any company, business, or industry that needs to sell a product. Other options include fundraising; working in the nonprofit sector; or working in an academic setting for an admissions, continuing education, development, or public relations office at a college or university. Employers will benefit from the contacts and connections you have made over the years in your previous career.

Many professionals turn their years of experience and expertise into a consulting business. Management, marketing, finance, information technology, or educational consulting are all good second-career choices.

Former public school teachers can turn to consulting work or educational sales. They can provide tutoring services or grant-writing services, or they can go on to educational administration. Their skill set enables them to teach at colleges or universities or find employment in nonprofit agencies or advising and counseling offices in colleges and universities. An English teacher, for example, could apply his or her skills to a second career as a magazine editor, a grant writer for a non-profit agency, or a freelance writer.

Health care career changers with a master's degree can find employment teaching at colleges, universities, or career and technical centers. They can also work as case reviewers for health insurance companies or the Social Security Administration; act as medical consultants to magazines, Web pages, or professional organizations; or write journal articles, newsletters, or books.

AGE-FRIENDLY OCCUPATIONS

Health care, education, and government are the top three industries that welcome older workers. Consulting and entrepreneurship are also popular options for older career changers.

The following occupations and industries have labor or skill shortages and have proven to be appropriate jobs for older workers, even those with disabilities or other limitations.

- Health care
- Education
- Accounting and Bookkeeper
- Administration and Clerical Work
- Business and Consulting
- Customer Service
- Financial Services
- Hospitality
- Real Estate
- Sales and Retail
- Transportation

There are several areas that promise great opportunities for Baby Boomers even in times of a recession. One of these areas is education. Many secondary teachers are expected to retire, leaving a gap in the supply of teachers. Going back to college and getting a teaching certificate can provide a fulfilling part-time or full-time position. Many states now offer special programs to speed up the certification process.

Financial services companies, banks, insurance companies, and real estate firms will value your networking experience and contacts, and they will tend to look beyond your age as long as you are still productive and energetic.

Older workers in sales, marketing, and consulting are especially attractive to employers because they can utilize the benefits of a mature work ethic and an area of expertise that can only come from years of experience. Colleges often hire older adults for full-time and adjunct teaching or to run various student services programs, or they hire older adults as staff members in the admissions, financial aid, business, career, and alumni relations office.

If you are unable to stand for long periods of time but enjoy the health care work environment, medical coding and billing, admissions, and health care administration positions are good office-based alternatives to nursing or other more physically demanding occupations.

If you possess excellent typing skills and speed, consider medical transcription or court reporting and captioning. These occupations lend themselves to lucrative part-time or even home-based employment if you have a home computer and an Internet connection.

ENCORE CAREERS

A relatively new term used to describe the Baby Boom generation's search for a career that offers personal meaning, *encore careers* refers to work that provides social impact and continued income. Coined by Marc Freedman, the term refers to careers that are neither retirement jobs nor a bridge between the end of employment and the beginning of retirement. Instead, they are an entire stage of life and work.[6] Freedman's nonprofit group, Civic Ventures (http://www.civicventures.org), helps people give back to their community while continuing to work productively.

A 2005 survey published by Civic Ventures and the MetLife Foundation surveyed 1,000 people ages 50 to 70.[7] The survey results showed that Boomers and pre-Boomers are ready for encore careers, for they:

- want to do work that helps others, now and in retirement
- want careers that are about people, purpose, and community
- have divergent attitudes about post-retirement work based on gender and race
- do not think it will be very easy to find second careers doing good work and strongly support public policy changes to remove obstacles

The results of the 2005 survey indicate a potentially good fit between the desires of a new generation of older Americans and some of the key sectors of society, namely, education, health care, and social services.

OUTSOURCE-PROOF OPTIONS

Jobs that are *prime candidates* for outsourcing overseas share the following characteristics:

- They have standards that are objective and easily assessed.
- They require little effort to share and learn the necessary knowledge and skills.
- They do not require direct physical contact with customers or colleagues.

Table 7.1
These jobs will *never* be outsourced

• Account/Customer Support	• Accounting & Finance Executive
• Administrative Assistant	• Auto Repair Technician
• Child Daycare Management	• Counseling/Social Work
• Database Administration	• Dental Assistant/Hygienist
• Diesel Mechanics	• Electrician
• Fitness Professional	• HVAC Technician
• Nurse	• Pharmacy Technician
• Plumber	• Restaurant/Banquet Services
• Retail Banker	• Sales Representative
• Testing/Quality Assurance	• Veterinary Assistant

The jobs that will *never* be outsourced are shown in Table 7.1.

RECESSION-PROOF CAREERS

All of us have heard stories of people being laid off from careers that one would have never thought would experience downsizing. In my state, even nurses have been laid off. In reality, there is no such thing as a recession-proof career, only those that are less prone to the effects of a recession.

Education is probably the least affected by the economy because public education at the elementary, middle, and high school levels is mandated. Even at the college level, faculty and staff positions are relatively secure as long as the college or university maintains a healthy enrollment. The next relatively recession-proof career is nursing, as is the health care field in general, because of the current shortage of nurses and the growing needs of our aging population.

ECONOMICS 101

It pays to observe economic trends to help determine which jobs will be in demand in the future and which ones will simply disappear.

Nursing is an interesting example of a career field dramatically affected by economic changes and simple supply and demand of the labor market. A series of significant events has occurred over the years that shaped the modern nursing profession into what it is today and contributed to the shortages we currently face.[8]

In the mid-1980s, the demand for nurses began to increase when legislation changed the Medicare reimbursement formula in 1983. At the same time, the supply of graduating nurses decreased because "nursing was judged to be too demanding, too undervalued, and too unrewarding."[9]

The increased number of older people in our population (aka Baby Boomers) created more demand for health care services in hospitals and home health care. Not enough graduates created a demand for nurses, which raised salaries. The recent downturn in the economy in 2008 caused fewer people to opt for medical procedures, which meant less profit for hospitals, which in turn resulted in a hiring freeze in many hospitals. This minor hiccup in job hiring does not mean there were no job openings, just a fewer number of openings and the disappearance of the lucrative sign-on bonuses graduates experienced just months ago. Nursing is still predicted to be a profession with an excellent future because of the rising proportion of people over age 65.

In addition, the average age of registered nurses (RNs) is projected to be 44.5 by 2012. Nurses in their fifties are expected to become the largest segment of the nursing workforce, accounting for almost one-quarter of the RN population.[10] When these nurses retire, there will simply not be younger replacements to fill their vacancies. The shortage of RNs in the United States is a real phenomenon and could reach as high as 500,000 by 2025.[11]

According to the *Careerism Report*, it pays to select a career where you function as a "doer" rather than as advisor or support worker.[12] Physicians and nurses are examples of "doers" because they perform a direct service, which is treating patients. Dieticians and nutritionists generally service in an advisory capacity. Likewise, those individuals who direct sell goods and services generally make more money than those who advise people about what to buy. Skilled construction workers or heavy equipment operators generally make more money than do estimators or computer-aided designers. Plumbers, electricians, roofers, heating and air-conditioning service people, and auto mechanics make more than office personnel, for example. Not only are such individuals highly trained in a specific job, theirs is a job that not everyone can do; and so when the service is needed, the cost is secondary (e.g., when your furnace goes out over the weekend).

Advising professions appear to be more vulnerable to economic conditions than "doers" because people tend to cut back on services that they can temporarily do without. Companies will cut back on training or business consultants; families will cut back on booking vacation trips to resorts, dining at fancy restaurants, getting tans, or other salon services.

LEVEL OF EDUCATION

In general, the more education or training required, the higher the salary. That is why the engineer, for example, receives a higher salary than the engineering technician—because the engineer has a higher level of training and more responsibility on the job than does the technician. Nurse anesthetists, who require a master's degree with extensive training in anesthesiology, can easily pull down a $100,000 salary.

People who hold a "professional degree," such as chiropractors, pharmacists, architects, attorneys, and veterinarians, usually command a greater salary than secretaries, general business managers, retail sales people, or elementary school teachers because of the length and difficulty of their post-baccalaureate training. The exceptions to this generality are those individuals who are at the top of their field (e.g., artists, actors, writers, and television broadcasting personalities).

TURN A HOBBY INTO A NEW CAREER

Wouldn't it be nice spending your day doing what you enjoy doing most? Do you have a passion for something, or do you have a natural talent? Do you want to do something that will make a difference in the lives of others such as work for a nonprofit group that educates children about good nutrition? Perhaps you always dreamed of opening a bed and breakfast, raising goats and selling natural soap products, or opening your own custom cabinet-making or interior design business?

Some of the most successful career changes come out of the desire to pursue a hobby. For example, consider a machinist who has a knack for creating specialty after-market engine parts for the sports car enthusiast. He begins by initially machining a few parts for friends and soon finds himself selling products on eBay and taking orders over the Internet. Later, once his business has grown, he has a guest column in a trade magazine and writes "how-to" manuals. The possibilities are endless!

Last year, I met with a woman who offers her office skills to companies for a fee. She provides typing, bookkeeping, and bulk mailing services and also fills in for receptionists and secretaries during vacations. The beauty of her services is that they essentially fill an outsourcing or temporary help niche for small companies.

Entrepreneurship can be an attractive option for many career changers. The opportunity to be your own boss, do what you enjoy, and set your own terms and schedule is an attractive option for people who have worked in a corporate structure for most of their lives.

If you are planning to start your own business, you must first come up with something to sell. Do you have a special skill that others may be willing to pay your fee for (computer database design, writing ability, or artistic ability, for example)? Do you possess knowledge or know processes and practices that can help others (management consultant to start-up businesses, marketing strategist, legal expertise provider, for example)? What assets do you have? Do you have a strong network of people who can become customers? Do you hold a positive reputation? Do you have access to customer or supply lists or marketing information?

There are only two things that your business can sell: a product or a service. Consider who will buy your product or service, why and how people will buy from you, where you will sell your product or service, and the price. Last, think about how you will promote your business to reach the greatest number of potential customers.

There are plenty of free services designed to assist new businesses regarding how to write a business plan and how to secure loans or funding for start-up costs. The Small Business Administration can be accessed online at www.smallbusiness.com. Many colleges and universities also offer free small business development services. Chambers of Commerce can also be a good source of assistance and can help promote your business and hook you up with business professionals in the area.

Only when you have created a sound business plan and are confident of your business's financial viability should you begin your new venture. Because most businesses fail within the first five years, you should have enough capital set aside for living and business expenses until profits begin to roll in. Consider working full-time or at least part-time at your current place of employment while developing your new business until it becomes self-sustaining, and then quit your job. Careful planning and listening to customer feedback will help you take some of the risk out of your business idea.

Home- or Internet-based business is less risky because such businesses have less overhead and fewer initial expenses. Working at home provides some attractive features for people who are tired of the administrative hierarchy in corporate American or the commute through heavy traffic. People who work from home need to be comfortable leaving the camaraderie of coworkers in an office setting and need to be able to separate or at least manage their time between business and family responsibilities.

Franchise businesses are attractive because they offer access to a proven business model and an established product. But as in any new business venture, it pays to do your homework before purchasing a franchise. Make sure that you fully understand the post-purchase costs that a franchise will incur, whether or not you have to purchase supplies solely from the franchise company, and be aware of the level of training, marketing, and resources available from the parent company.

Chapter 8

CAREERS TO CONSIDER

The best way to predict the future is to create it.

Peter Drucker

If you are unclear or undecided in what direction to take your future career change, I recommend first looking at careers in broad categories and then narrowing down your choices. *Career clusters* are broad occupational categories that group careers according to common characteristics.[1] Examples of career clusters are Art, Business, Education, Health Science, and Human Service. All the careers in the Health Science cluster, for example, share a common job characteristic of helping or treating people; they also involve science or medicine. Yet the Health Science cluster is broad enough to include a number of occupational choices ranging from phlebotomy, nursing, and medical laboratory technology to professional degrees like speech pathology, pharmacy, or anesthesiology.

The career cluster method lets career explorers quickly sort through the thousands of occupations that exist in the world, discard the occupational clusters they have no real interest in pursuing, and focus on one or two areas that still contain a variety of choices. Traditionally, the career cluster concept has been used to group occupations and industries and identify academic pathways from secondary schools to two- and four-year colleges. Because I work in a college setting, I organize my career clusters by college and major, a slightly different way than the standard 16 career clusters listed at www.careerclusters.org.

AGRICULTURE AND NATURAL RESOURCES

Do you have a green thumb?
Do you enjoy working with plants and animals?
Are you passionate about protecting the environment?
Do you enjoy an outdoor work environment?

Description: Occupations in the Agriculture and Natural Resources career cluster can be divided into the following categories: agribusiness management, agricultural and natural resources communications, building construction management, parks recreation and tourism resources, packaging, horticulture, forestry, food science, and fisheries and wildlife.

Sample Occupations: Food scientist, forest ranger, environmental engineer, agriculture teacher, animal scientist, animal breeder, biochemist, genetic scientist, horticulturist, food safety specialist, park manager, geologist, landscaper, fish and game warden, logger, veterinarian, veterinary assistant, and turf grass manager.

Tip: Agriculture generates over 22 million jobs in the United States, and most of them are located near or associated with farms. See www.agriculturalcareers.com for a complete listing of careers.

ART

Are you visually oriented?
Do you have a natural talent for acting, writing, drawing, dancing, or playing an instrument?
Do you like to perform or interpret music?
Is artistic expression important to you?
Do you enjoy the freedom of creating something new?

Description: The Art cluster is composed of such creative disciplines as drawing, painting, sculpture, graphic design, photography, creative and technical writing, journalism, theater, dance, and music.

Sample Occupations:

Visual Arts: Art instructor, fashion designer, sculptor, painter, photographer, animator, commercial artist, set designer, and interior decorator.

Performing Arts: The Performing Arts occupations include not only performers but also all the behind-the-scenes workers who make performances possible. Among such workers are production managers, cinematographers, dancers, playwrights, directors, actors, make-up artists, costume designers, theater directors, set designers, sound effects technicians, stage lighting technicians, musicians, music teachers, composers, and conductors.

Tip: It may be difficult to establish oneself as an artist initially. Many people pursue a teaching credential while they are cultivating commissions or preparing for a galley exhibit. The Internet has helped artists of all mediums showcase and advertise work and services. In many art-related professions, a portfolio is critical to showcase your creative and technical skills.

BUSINESS

Are you good at working with other people?
Are you a natural leader?
Are you entrepreneurial?
Do you have a talent for organizing and planning?
Do you enjoy working with numbers?
Do you feel confident handling other people's money?
Are you precise, responsible, and creative?

Description: Occupations in the Business and Administration career cluster involve planning, organizing, directing, performing, and evaluating business functions that are essential to effective and productive business operations.

Sample Occupations:

Banking: Loan officer, teller, compliance officer, credit analyst, new accounts clerk, internal auditor, bill collector, mortgage underwriter, and customer service representative.

Business Analysis: Management consultant, actuarial scientist, management analyst, operations analyst, systems analyst, and business analyst.

Administrative and Information Support: Receptionist, secretary, mail clerk, information systems manager, transcriptionist, database manager, office manager, and records clerk.

Financial Management and Accounting: Auditor, accountant, bookkeeping clerk, financial analyst, financial planner, stockbroker, treasurer, tax preparer, tax examiner, controller, economist, auditor, development officer, real estate asset manager, securities underwriter, and securities sales agent.

Human Resources: These occupations focus on the management of people and include labor relations manager, personnel manager, organizational psychologist, and human resources manager.

Insurance Services: Actuary, insurance underwriter, insurance appraiser, claims agent, claims adjuster, insurance agent, and claims investigator.

Management: Administrative manager, restaurant manager, hotel manager, marketing manager, advertising manager, small business entrepreneur, and retail manager.

Marketing and Communications: Marketing assistant, market researcher, marketing manager, marketing director, public relations specialist, product developer, and promotions manager.

COMMUNICATIONS

Are you interested in working in television, film, or radio?
Do you like to work with technology?
Do you have a talent for writing?
Do you enjoy the limelight?
Are you tenacious?

Description: Occupations in the Communications career cluster include all the methods by which we communicate, including the visual and performing arts, journalism, writing, radio and television broadcasting, public relations, speech communication, and advertising.

Sample Occupations:

Audio and Video Technology: Audio systems technician, technical computer support technician for stage or screen, audiovideo engineer, computer graphics animator, and video systems technician.

Journalism and Broadcasting: Control room technician, station manager, radio and TV announcer, editor, reporter, anchor, broadcast technician, and production manager.

Telecommunications Technologies: Telecommunications technician, cable installer, telephone line repairer, and telecommunications computer programmer.

Printing Technology: Printing equipment operator, lithographer, desktop publishing specialist, graphic design artist, and Web page designer.

Writing: Author, poet, editor, publisher, copyeditor, freelance writer, technical writer, advertising manager, copywriter, speechwriter, and public relations staff.

EDUCATION

Do you enjoy teaching others?
Are you patient?
Are you comfortable with public speaking?
Are you creative?
Do you enjoy working with children or teenagers?
Do you enjoy helping people learn new skills?
Are you outgoing?

Description: The Education career cluster includes all the jobs involved in teaching or training students and adults in settings from preschool to college to business conference rooms.

Sample Occupations: Teacher (public, private, secondary, or post-secondary), teacher's aide, industry trainer, educational consultant, tutor, child care director, child care worker, child development specialist, early childhood teacher, superintendent, principal, instructional coordinator, education researcher, college president, curriculum developer, and instructional media designer.

Tip: Alternative teacher certification is a good option for career changers who hold bachelor's degrees to begin teaching without standard certification. Most states have provisions for alternative or emergency certification so they can hire uncertified teachers temporarily. The emergency option allows individuals to complete their certification by attending graduate school part-time while working. Also keep in mind that many private and parochial schools do not require certification.[2]

ENGINEERING AND CONSTRUCTION

Are you good at making designs or models?
Can you visualize projects in your mind?
Do you enjoy building and fixing things?
Are you good with plans and blueprints?
Do you enjoy math and physics?

Description: The Engineering and Construction career cluster includes those occupations related to the design, installation, or building of machines, buildings, products, or processes. Construction workers are involved in all phases of building highways, cities, homes, bridges, and waterways. Engineers research and develop solutions to technical problems by applying the theories and principles of science and mathematics.

Sample Occupations:

Engineering: Systems engineer, safety engineer, chemical engineer, transportation engineer, optical engineer, nuclear engineer, mechanical engineer, industrial engineer, electrical engineer, civil engineer, biotechnology engineer, and agricultural engineer.

Preconstruction and Design: These occupations include all the jobs done before a project can be built, including architect, civil engineer, computer-aided drafting and design technician, cost estimator, contractor, developer, highway engineer, surveyor, specifications writer, and urban planner.

Construction: These occupations include all the jobs involved in actual construction, from demolition to finished carpentry. Jobs include bricklayer, construction worker, demolition worker, heavy equipment operator, drywall installer, mason, floor covering installer, pipefitter, and welder.

Maintenance and Operations: These occupations involve maintaining, repairing, and upgrading structures. Jobs include electrician; plumber; painter; heating, ventilation, and air-conditioning (HVAC) technician; building inspector; and architectural historian.

HEALTH CARE

Do you enjoy helping people feel better?
Are you interested in medicine or dentistry?
Would you enjoy teaching people how to live a healthy lifestyle?
Do you pay attention to small details?
Do you have an excellent memory?
Would you like working in a hospital or other medical facility?

Description: Health Care is a very broad cluster that contains the medical sciences, therapy services for people with various ailments, wellness, nutrition, and personal care.

Sample Occupations:

Information and Communication Services: Workers in these occupations are responsible for managing and organizing health information. Occupations include admitting clerk, medical records administrator, hospital administrator, medical transcriptionist, medical coder, medical biller, and health educator.

Diagnostic Services: These occupations are involved in administering tests to diagnose diseases and disorders. Radiologist, cytotechnologist, sonographer, dialysis technician, blood bank technologist, medical technician, phlebotomist, and medical laboratory technician.

Therapeutic Services: These occupations provide treatment and therapy for diseases and disorders. Jobs include emergency medical technician (EMT)/paramedic, physician, physician assistant, registered nurse, dentist, pharmacist, physical therapist, speech and language pathologist, occupational therapist, chiropractor, optometrist, audiologist, respiratory therapist, speech and language pathologist, surgical technologist, dental assistant, dental hygienist, and certified nurse assistant.

Health and Wellness: Coach, athletic trainer, golf professional, activities director, dietician, wellness coach, physical trainer, health education teacher, chiropractor, and massage therapist.

Tip: Health care is one of the fastest-growing occupations and contains something for everyone. Many people think all health careers involve direct patient care. Fortunately, there are many interesting, rewarding health careers that require little or no patient contact. If you like science, you could become a clinical laboratory technician or a pharmaceutical scientist. If you are well organized and like being in charge, think about a career in health care administration. Are you good with math? There is a big demand for specialists in informatics. Public Health is another field that offers a wide variety of career possibilities. Even artists can find work in the health field as medical illustrators.

The aging of America will increase demand for a wide range of health care workers. Geriatric health care providers include doctors, pharmacists, mental health professionals, nurses, occupational and speech therapists, and other allied health workers who have completed advanced training in caring for older patients.

HOSPITALITY CAREERS

Do you enjoy travel?
Do you like to cook?
Do you want to help other people enjoy themselves?
Are you friendly and outgoing?
Would you like to work in a hotel, on a cruise ship, or in a restaurant?

Description: Hospitality careers encompass the hotel, restaurant, tourism, and leisure activity industry.

Sample Occupations: Chef, cook, baker, pastry artist, travel agent, hotel manager, food services manager, leisure and entertainment manager, golf club manager, ski lodge director, tennis instructor, tour director, cruise ship director, gaming manager, concierge, blackjack dealer, and convention manager.

COUNSELING AND HUMAN SERVICES CAREERS

Do you enjoy helping other people?
Are you sympathetic to people in unfortunate situations?
Do you like to help people feel better and improve their lives?

Description: The Counseling and Human Services cluster includes occupations that apply mental health, psychological, or human development principles to helping individuals, families, groups, and communities with issues related to wellness, personal growth, adjustment, career, or treatment of pathology.

Sample Occupations: Counselor, psychologist, psychiatrist, social worker, geriatric counselor, psychiatric aide, art therapist, marriage and family therapist, career counselor, substance abuse counselor, crisis counselor, mental health aide, sociologist, public health social worker, social service case management aide or assistant, residential program technician, community support or outreach worker, and mental health technician.

INFORMATION TECHNOLOGY

Do you enjoy working with computers?
Are you fascinated by technology?
Are you a logical and mathematical learner?
Are you organized and detail-oriented?
Do you learn new computer programs easily?
Do you love books or looking up information on the Internet?
Do you adapt well to change?

Description: The Information Technology career cluster involves the design, development, support, and management of hardware, software multimedia, and systems integration services. This cluster also includes library and information sciences.

Sample Occupations:

Information Support and Services: This group of occupations involves analyzing users' requirements in detail, selecting the best possible solution, writing specifications, and obtaining the necessary hardware. Jobs include data systems designer, help desk technician, application integrator, technical writer, database specialist, data analyst, and maintenance technician.

Programming and Software Development: People in this group of occupations design, develop, and produce computer software. Occupations include systems analyst, programmer, business analyst, operating systems designer, software architect, software engineer, and applications analyst.

Network Systems: This group of occupations includes the workers who establish and maintain links between computers, either within a single office, or across the Internet. Occupations include wireless area network (WAN) and local area network (LAN) technician, communications analyst, systems engineer, network support specialist, network engineer, network administrator, and personal computer (PC) support specialist.

Interactive Media: Webmaster, Web designer, digital media specialist, and multimedia author.

Library Information Services: Librarian, reference librarian, children's librarian, medical librarian, and instructional technologist.

LEGAL

Do you respect the law?
Do you like to help people?

Do you think it would be exciting to work in a courtroom?
Are you good at debating and winning arguments?
Are you detail-oriented and driven?
Would you enjoy being responsible for other people's safety?

Description: The Legal cluster involves careers in forensics, corrections, homeland security, law enforcement, and the judicial process.

Sample Occupations:

Law and Legal Public Services: Legislator, judge, magistrate, attorney, legal assistant and paralegal, court reporter, and inspector or compliance officer.

Criminal Justice and Corrections: Security guard, forensic expert, police chief, police officer, detective, corrections officer, bailiff, probation officer, FBI agent, court advocate, security guard, private investigator, and U.S. marshal.

GOVERNMENT AND PUBLIC SERVICES

Do you value public service?
Are you interested in government and politics?
Would you like to work overseas?

Description: Occupations in the Government and Public Services career cluster involve planning, managing, and providing legislative, administrative, and regulatory services at the federal, state, and local levels.

Sample Occupations: Bill collector, government official, firefighter, military, museum curator, tour director, genealogist, commissioner, legislator, mayor, urban or regional planner, budget analyst, and recreation and parks director.

SCIENCE AND MATH

Do you enjoy science?
Are you good at math?
Do you want to find answers to questions?
Would you enjoy working in a laboratory?
Are you detail-oriented?

Description: The Science and Math cluster involves scientific and mathematics research, application, laboratory and testing services, and new product development.

Sample Occupations: Biologist, chemist, physicist, astronomer, oceanographer, marine biologist, meteorologist, botanist, zoologist, entomologist, geneticist, microbiologist, teacher, medical or scientific researcher, quality controller, toxicologist, forensic scientist, physicist, anthropologist, physiologist, archeologist, mathematician, and statistician.

Tip: There is a nationwide push to encourage more people to enter science- and math-related careers because of the severe shortage of scientist, engineers, and researchers in America.

TRANSPORTATION, DISTRIBUTION, AND LOGISTICS

Are you organized and efficient?
Do you have good eyesight and quick reflexes?
Are you good at solving problems?
Are you good at understanding mechanics?

Description: The Transportation, Distribution, and Logistics career cluster involves the planning, management, and movement of people, materials, and goods by road, air, rail, and water.

Sample Occupations: Airplane pilot, aircraft mechanic, stewardess, diesel mechanic, dispatcher, logistics expert, auto mechanic, automotive sales associate, inspector, freight handler, merchant marine, railroad mechanic, signals operator, taxi driver, truck driver, warehouse supervisor, and forklift driver.

GREEN CAREERS

The "green" movement looks like it's here to stay. Our concern for saving our planet and using renewable and earth-friendly resources will create many opportunities for individuals interested in careers in alternative fuel development, clean energy, solar and wind engineering, ecology, environmental journalism, sustainable architecture, organic horticulture, environmental education, and environmental management work for sustainable nonprofit organizations.

Job opportunities should also be abundant for environmental, chemical, mechanical, and electrical engineers; solar energy technicians; wind power technicians; and architects who have qualified for Leadership in Energy and Environmental Design (LEED) certification. As well, HVAC technicians, who have been in demand for years, should likewise benefit from the push to "go green" by making buildings more energy-efficient and environmentally safe and sound.

NONPROFIT ORGANIZATIONS

Nonprofit organizations are tax-exempt, nongovernmental entities that are organized and operate exclusively for one or more of the following purposes: religious, charitable, scientific, testing for public safety, literacy, educational, fostering national or international amateur sports competition, or the prevention of cruelty to children or animals.[3] Nonprofit organizations can provide excellent opportunities for midlife career changers.

Most nonprofits fall into the following 10 major categories:[4]

1. Arts, Culture, and Humanities
2. Education

3. Environment and Animals
4. Health
5. Human Services
6. International, Foreign Affairs
7. Public, Societal Benefit
8. Religion Related
9. Mutual or Membership Benefit
10. Unknown, Unclassified

Types of nonprofit organizations include soup kitchens, homeless shelters, clinics, museums, zoos, the Gates Foundation, libraries, churches, the Society for the Prevention of Cruelty to Animals (SPCA), and the Red Cross and represent every cause or passion imaginable. Employees of nonprofits are housewives, corporate executives, professionals, and PhDs. The range of pay is unpaid to lucrative. People like to work in nonprofit organizations because doing so gives them a sense of purpose, meaning, and of working toward a common goal. Many career changers find that the desire to make a change in the lives of those they may help, whether in the local community or the rest of the world, is worth the effort to make the transition. The mission-driven culture is much different from a corporate culture, for the quality of people, and the passion they bring to their work,[5] creates a cohesive and rewarding place to work. Types of jobs are advocacy, fundraising, technology, lobbying, research, event planning, volunteer coordination, and grant writing.

The benefits to working in the nonprofit sector are the family-friendly atmosphere, flexible hours, ability to contribute to society in your day job, and room for creativity. The downsides are financial constraints, lack of pay, and the amount of work (many nonprofit workers wear more than one hat). Jobs are found through ads in papers, personal networking, and volunteering.

OCCUPATIONAL RESEARCH

Once you have identified one or two broad career areas, the next step is to research individual occupations. Because there are literally thousands of career opportunities to choose from in today's world, using the Internet can make your research easier by providing instant, up-to-date career information from sources all over the world. The Internet is a powerful and efficient tool that can help you make a better, more informed career decision from the comfort of your home at any time of the day or night.

With all this information at our fingertips, how do we know which Web sites to use? I usually use Web sites authored by professional organizations, governmental agencies, nonprofit organizations, or colleges or universities. Sites from such sources tend to be well established and reputable.

An easy way to begin searching for information about careers is to do a simple Google search. Simply type "careers in [e.g., Accounting]" in your Internet search box for a list of the most popular and relevant Web sites containing information about that career. Another excellent source of career information is the O*NET Online at http://online.onetcenter.org or America's Career InfoNet, which can be found at http://www.acinet.org/acinet/.

As you research occupations, try to gather the following information:

1. What exactly does a person in this career do on a daily basis?
2. What is the typical work environment for this career?
3. What are the average earnings for this career? Look at the starting salary as well as the high and low salary range.
4. What are the minimal entry level requirements for this profession? What educational degree, training, certification, licensing, or skills are required? Are there any special personal attributes, mental capacities, or physical requirements needed to perform the job tasks in this career?
5. What are the positive and negative aspects of this career?
6. What is the future job outlook for this career? Will there be a demand for this occupation five or ten years from now, or is the industry subject to economic fluctuations or local labor market demand?

This is your time to investigate all the career possibilities and to be open-minded. You may be very clear on what you would like to change your career to, or your idea may still be a little fuzzy and unfocused. Plan you transition in such a way that you have a bit of flexibility. You may not know which specific science discipline you want to pursue, but that will come as you start investigating science careers and begin taking classes and are exposed to all the opportunities available in that field. Take the first step toward your next career. Happy exploring!

Chapter 9

MAKE A PLAN *BEFORE* YOU QUIT YOUR JOB

Life isn't about finding yourself. Life is about creating yourself.

George Bernard Shaw

In our ever-changing economic times, it is difficult to plan what will happen next week, let alone try to peer into the future and predict what we will be doing five years from now. However, that does not mean you should jump into a career change without any thought given to the consequences. My approach to career planning is to plan for the future as much as you realistically can, but leave your plan flexible enough to take advantage of any opportunities that may arise, and revise your plans accordingly. This flexible planning perspective may appear contradictory at first, but the circuitous nature is more reflective of today's modern career development. Traditional career development theories and models ascribed to a linear process of self-reflection, exploration, and implementation. Given the unpredictable nature of today's economy and life events, we need to modify that approach to include active exploration, revision in the face of life's sudden unpredictable changes, and the openness and flexibility to be able to take advantage of any unexpected opportunities that rise.

Making some kind of career plan, however sketchy, *before* you quit your job reduces the risk involved in making a career change and allows career changers the necessary time to understand themselves, explore possible career options, and set in place a series of future actions that will increase the chances of making a successful career change. Sometimes being fired or laid off can be a great motivator to search for a new job or create a new career. However, unless you really need that level of motivation, the safest way to plan a career change is while you are still employed because it simply gives you more options. So take your future in your hands, and do not wait for external factors to force you to make a change before you are ready and have the resources in place to be successful.

BRAD

"I'm 55 years old and I just can't do it anymore!" Brad was working in a warehouse distribution center at the time but did not enjoy his job anymore for several reasons: the climate at work had changed, there was no room to advance, and he

was tired of driving the 37-mile commute. *"I used to work in customer service, and I did it because I needed to, but that's not what I want to do now. The time is right for me to do something." "When you're younger, you let other things get in the way; but then you get to a point where you say, enough, and it's time to do something else."*

Brad decided to go to school full-time for a few months to earn a pharmacy technician degree rather than spend years pursuing another degree part-time. After he graduated, Brad's goal was to get a job closer to home and, depending on the company's tuition reimbursement policy, maybe go back to school to finish a paramedic degree (Brad was a volunteer EMT for his township). Brad calculated the cost of tuition and fees and determined it was within his means. He also researched the salary potential and discovered that he would be making the same or better salary as he was now but would have more potential for advancement or movement than he does now. Brad did his research by talking with several pharmacy technicians at his local pharmacy. In looking at his work values and career interests, he saw that Pharmacy Technology was a good match because he really liked the medical aspect, he could utilize his previous customer service skills, and the career would give him some growth options. Brad concluded the session by saying, *"I guess I had a plan but I just didn't know it. I'm grateful I have a job, but does that mean I shouldn't look for something else?"* In Brad's case, this was exactly the time to plan for a new opportunity—while he is still employed.

Many people jump from one job to another out of desperation only to find themselves ending up in an equally unsatisfying situation. Use the time while you are still employed to ask yourself what you really want out of life and to plan out your next career move. Put your dreams into a realistic, attainable format and problem-solve ways to reach beyond any initial limitations or "bumps in the road." No one is asking you to become a professional dancer if you have two left feet. However, if you possess the desire and a degree of natural talent, perhaps you could develop a plan to increase your technical skills by taking dance lessons at night, work toward earning a teaching degree in dance, or even opening your own dance studio.

Explore Your Options

Make a list of all the different types of positions you could get with the skills, education, and work experience you currently possess. Then ask yourself the following questions:

1. Are you interested in upgrading your education?
2. What kind of job can you get with more education?
3. What do you have to do to obtain more education?
4. Should you search for another job?
5. What would be involved in searching for a new job?
6. Should you start your own business?
7. Should you retire?
8. If you retired, what steps would be required?

If you are planning to start your own business, translating passion into profit is the challenge. Get the facts and dig beyond the myths of entrepreneurism. Granted, working for yourself may offer more freedom, but the hours are usually longer. You will also need to determine if you have what it takes to succeed in a competitive business world.

Exercise 1: The Career Changer's Inventory
Education: _____

Current Job: _____

Skills: _____

Previous Job: _____

Skills: _____

Interests and Hobbies: _____
_____

What would it take to make your wishes come true?

_____ Upgrade skills		_____ Work for self
_____ Reenter workforce		_____ Different job
_____ Reduce workload		_____ New career
_____ Volunteer or not work		_____ Other (explain)

Constraints (realities): _____
_____
_____

Can any of these constraints be modified? _____
_____

Is there a way to try out your new career to see if it's right for you *before* quitting your job? _____
    Next Steps:
    1. _____
    2. _____
    3. _____
    4. _____

KEEP YOUR GOALS SIMPLE

For maximum success in your career change, keep your goals simple. It's fine to begin with a dream or vision, but then get down to the basics and fill in the gaps with step-by-step details. Proceed forward in small reachable goals, so you do not become discouraged. Review and revise your plans accordingly, but keep moving forward.

Planning Steps

1. If you have not done so already, investigate career possibilities or refer to the "Get the Facts" section in Chapter 6. Research the feasibility of making a career change to a particular field.

2. Plan your career transition. Will you need to go to school or training, or can you obtain the skills you need on the job, through volunteer work, or by sampling your new career through a part-time or temporary position? If schooling is required, how much schooling will you need, and how long will it take? Can you realistically obtain the required skills and credentials? What certifications or licensing requirements are necessary? Detail how you will finance your career change. If, for example, you are considering going back to school for a career in nursing or engineering that has competitive entrance requirements, you may want to generate a contingency plan. Acknowledge the challenges and obstacles you may face, whether your age, education, or current financial obligations, and develop ways to overcome these challenges. List the steps required to complete each goal along the way. Include a timeline for applying to school, graduating, writing your resume, researching the job market, and applying for positions.

3. Budget for your career transition. Include the costs of education or training and fees for certification or licensing exams, living expenses, and travel while going to school; costs of membership dues for professional organizations, subscriptions to trade journals, or any travel- or business-related costs associated with interviewing or relocating.

Kendra

After years of working as a marketing professional, Kendra made the decision to go back to school to become a registered nurse. After researching the requirements for a RN degree by talking with an admissions counselor at her local community college, Kendra discovered that she could transfer in the "general" or "core" courses from her previous bachelor's degree in marketing. She would have to pick up two anatomy and physiology courses and developmental psychology. Taking into consideration that her program contained competitive admissions requirements, it would take her about two and a half years to complete her degree. The nursing program she wanted to attend was available on a full-time basis during the daytime or on a part-time basis during the evening. After talking with instructors and former students, Kendra decided to enroll in the daytime program not only to shorten the time she would be in school but also because her instructors told her that the academic intensity of the program was not conducive to holding a full-time job while attending school. Kendra planned to pick up all of the prerequisite courses on a part-time basis, at night, in the spring and summer semesters before she quit her position at work and began her full-time day series of nursing courses.

To finance her education, Kendra decided to apply for financial aid and dipped into her savings to cover the rest of the expenses. Luckily for Kendra, her husband had a job that could sustain them while she went to school. In her sophomore year, she applied for a full-tuition scholarship that would pay for the costs of tuition and books in return for an employment commitment at her local hospital. This alleviated some of the financial pressure while solving the issue of finding a job once she graduated.

The benefits of Kendra's career change: more money, better job opportunities, and the chance to work directly with people in a caretaking role. The costs of Kendra's career change: time and money. Going back to school for two and a half years meant some financial sacrifice as well as less time to spend with her family.

FINANCING YOUR CAREER CHANGE

Making a career change is not easy, particularly in midlife when you have built up years of experience, a particular lifestyle, certain tastes and expectations, expenses, and social status. Be aware of the financial considerations involved in making a career change, and allow the necessary time to plan for the transition, acquire the proper resources, and look for a new job. Lastly, be prepared to experience a drop in income as you reestablish yourself financially.

Programs such as Volunteers in Service (VISTA) or the Peace Corps can get you started in a new career while providing you with a modest living allowance. So can graduate or research assistantships, which allow you to complete graduate school while receiving a stipend for teaching courses or conducting research. Such other programs as *Americorps* (www.americorps.org) and *Teach for America* (www.teachforamerica.org) will "forgive" student loans for teachers who agree to teach in underserved areas of the country. Public schools in rural or inner-city areas that have severe teacher shortages will often hire individuals to teach while paying for a substantial portion of the cost of their earning an education degree. Examples are California's *EnCorps Teacher Initiative* for math and science professionals, and the Pentagon's *Troops to Teachers* program for military and enlisted personnel. Many hospitals offer nursing scholarship programs that will cover tuition and living expenses in return for an employment commitment after graduation.

Even if you cannot get your schooling paid up front through tuition reimbursement or government programs, you may be able to receive a tax break for the cost of schooling. You may, for example, be able to claim a Hope and Lifetime Learning Credit for tuition and related expenses if you are enrolled in an eligible educational institution. You may also be able to claim a tuition deduction of up to $4,000 and be able to deduct the interest you pay on a qualified student loan. See the "Tax Incentives for Higher Education" page of the Internal Revenue Service (IRS) Web site at www.irs.gov.

There are a variety of tax incentives for education; among them are after-tax college saving accounts. With help from your financial advisor, it may be possible to use a portion of your portfolio to create a "retirement income" or other type of annuity that pays out living expenses over a period of time while you return to school.

Dᴇᴄʀᴇᴀsᴇ Rɪsᴋ Wʜᴇɴ Mᴀᴋɪɴɢ ᴀ Cᴀʀᴇᴇʀ Cʜᴀɴɢᴇ

You need to be comfortable taking a risk and pushing yourself beyond your comfort level to reach something new. Of course, the safest way to make a career transition is to keep one foot in your job while strategically preparing or positioning yourself for the move. Here are some ways to minimize the amount of risk involved in making a career change:

- Do all your research about your future career.
- Talk to people (informational interviewing) who are already in the career you plan to change to and ask them what they like, do not like, the risks, the rewards, and how they got started, and so on.
- Get a mentor to help you transition into the new field and learn some of the tricks of the trade.
- Try out a new career on a trial basis by working part-time in a new industry or by using a sabbatical or vacation time to explore other options. This method allows you to learn new skills or test the waters in a new career without leaving the safety of your permanent job. You can create a transition plan into your full-time new career later. Develop a timetable for acquiring new skills.
- When establishing your new career on a secondary or part-time basis, try to find a job that is near your home or place of full-time employment to minimize travel, late hours, and pressure. While you are planning your career change, you want to continue to be a strong contributor in your primary position.
- Start your new business venture on a part-time basis from your home while still maintaining your primary job. Be careful using work time to conduct personal business. Your boss will not be happy to hear you are making money off the company's Internet, fax, or existing customers. Be careful about such direct conflicts of interest as using existing customers or working for competitors. When your home business, for example, is healthy enough to generate enough income on a full-time basis, then you can begin the process of leaving your primary position and establishing your home business on a full-time basis.

Some people take small incremental steps over a period of years, refining their career plan and progressing through a series of related jobs until they reach their desired position or career.

Research by Herminia Ibarra indicates that trying out different jobs, or testing possible future careers, is the way to begin making a career change. Ibarra argues that to reinvent yourself, you must live through a period of transition in which you must rethink and reconfigure a multitude of possibilities.[1]

Research can take you only so far, though, especially if you are planning to change your career to an unfamiliar field. Once you have done as much research-ing about your future career as humanely possible, then you must take the next step through direct involvement in your future profession. Try to obtain some real-world experience by taking classes, volunteering, interviewing a professional in the field, job shadowing, or even trying a part-time or temporary position before committing yourself to your new career.

If you are planning to make a career change to a related industry that does not require going back to school to earn a degree or certification, your greatest chal-lenge will be finding an employer who will take a chance on hiring you with no experience. To decrease the perceived risk from an employer, take an interim step that can get you closer to your goal and increase your skill set. If you work for a large organization, you can even look for opportunities to move to another depart-ment or even be mentored. Your current employer is more likely to take the risk of developing you for a new career because you are a known quantity. If you are missing a piece of experience, one way to gain that experience or acquire new skills is to volunteer your services to a particular company or organization. Say, "I'll do a marketing project for you'" or "I'll do a C++ project for you for free," and then do it and put it on your resume. Each step you take moves you closer to your intended goal.

I was working in the admissions department at a small college when I decided that I wanted to make a transition into academic advising. Having no real previ-ous experience in that area, I volunteered to help out with freshman orientation in the summer and late registration when classes began in the fall semester. I not only received the training I needed, but my actions also let my supervisors know that I was interested in this type of move. So when some organizational restructur-ing occurred on campus as a result of budget cuts, I was transferred to a job in the advising center.

If you are planning to go back to school, you do not necessarily need to change your major to shift your career in another direction. Many professional de-velopment opportunities, like continuing education courses or workshops, can provide the extra edge. If your goal is to land a supervisory position, a few man-agement courses may be beneficial. Or, if your computer skills need upgrading, a Microsoft Office course may help.

WHEN YOU ARE FORCED TO MAKE A CAREER CHANGE

Sometimes situations occur that force people to make an unplanned, or unwanted, career change. A company closing, downsizing, layoff, firing, or injury or disability can suddenly result in the need to find a new line of work. Your choices are to transition to a related line of work or start fresh in an entirely new career field. The challenges are to adjust to the sudden emotional upheaval of losing your job and your career identify and salvaging the years of training and experience you have accumulated and transforming it into a new occupation.

To begin this process, complete the following worksheet:

Exercise 2: Recently Unemployed, Laid Off, or Downsized Workers

1. What is your current situation?

   _____

2. Identify your skills and experience.

   _____

3. Identify your options.
   a. Find another job. (What kind of job can you get with what you have?)

   _____

   b. Upgrade your skills. (What kind of job can you get with more education?)

   _____

   c. Go back to school for a new career. (What kind of job and salary can you expect to get in your new field?) _____
   Will you need to return to school if you change careers? _____
   d. Start your own business. (What type of business? Do you have or can you obtain the necessary start-up materials and financing?) _____
   e. Retire. (What is the feasibility of retiring? What would you need to do?)

   _____

4. What are your priorities? (What do you need to do now versus later?)
   1. _____
   2. _____
   3. _____
5. What are the obstacles or constraints? Problem-solve solutions to any obstacles by identifying the obstacle and suggesting a possible solution.
   Obstacle　　　　　　　　　　　Solution
   1. _____　　　_____
   2. _____　　　_____
   3. _____　　　_____
6. What do you need to do to prepare yourself for the option you have chosen? Obtain skills? Write a resume? Investigate jobs? Research careers? Look for job openings?

   _____

   _____

7. Develop a career or educational plan of action. List the tasks you need to complete or steps you need to take to reach your goal.
   1. _____
   2. _____
   3. _____
   4. _____
   5. _____

Taking the time to plan and prepare for your next career is a wise investment in your future. Just like setting up a financial retirement plan, the thought you put into your next career move will reap huge dividends—especially if it allows you to be happy while working longer.

The following is a good illustration of the type of career strategizing that one needs to do to develop a feasible career plan for the future. In this example, Susan decided to make a career transition to a related profession rather than a complete career change.

Susan

Susan was a single woman in her mid-forties when she was laid off from her graphic design job of eight years. "I feel like I'm at a crossroads. I have two options: upgrade my skills or change careers by possibly going into teaching," she initially told me over the phone. After discussing her current situation, Susan admitted that she really enjoyed her profession and really could not see herself doing anything else. Susan's strong points were that she already had a bachelor's degree and a killer portfolio. However, her biggest concern was that she would not be able to work the same way she did before (a 9-to-5 permanent position with benefits for one company). She stated that companies seem to be cutting back to a skeleton crew and only want to hire designers on an as-needed basis. Since she mentioned an interest in teaching and already had a bachelor's degree in Fine Arts, I asked her if she had ever considered teaching before now. Susan said she originally considered high school teaching but was concerned about the number of art and music programs being eliminated from the public school systems in our area. I asked her if she had ever considered teaching at the college level, which would require at least a master's degree (about two years of schooling either way). After checking into the feasibility of teaching art or graphics at the high school level, she decided that the college environment might be more suitable as well as more interesting.

Since Susan obviously enjoyed her work and was very talented, I suggested she find a way to continue to stay in her profession. We explored the possibility of developing a freelance business. The Internet would allow her to expand her business beyond the boundaries of her geographic location. She was concerned about finding a job that provided benefits. We discussed the possibility of being able to make enough money on a freelance basis to afford health care or the possibility that one of her commissioned contacts may lead to a full-time position.

Susan had been on several interviews, and from those experiences she learned that she needed to update her computer graphics and Web page—programming skills. She had a great interview with a broadcasting communications company, whose interviewer was very impressed with her range of skills and previous work but was looking for someone with video editing experience. So now Susan knows what she needs to do to position herself for this type of job in the future.

Susan's Plan A is to continue to look for a permanent position. Plan B is to supplement her income with freelance assignments in the meantime while picking up specific computer graphics and Web design courses over the next few semesters. If she obtains a position, she will still continue to go to school to update her skills and maybe even pursue a master's degree to qualify for a college teaching job (Plan C). To help her increase the chances of finding employment, I suggested she "cold call" industries that have marketing departments, such as banks and financial institutions, or contact companies that sell their products online or have a strong Web presence. She realized the need to "think out of the box" for employment opportunities and go beyond her comfort zone to find or create them. Having a Plan A and a Plan B (and even a Plan C) provides her with more options in an uncertain future.

REFLECT ON AND REVISE YOUR PLAN

Your career plan is a work in progress, to be refined and honed as often as necessary. Because there is an element of unpredictability in planning for the future, you may have to tolerate some ambiguity along your career journey. Depending on what your circumstances are, you may have to develop a Plan A and a Plan B or a series of incremental steps to finally reach your goal.

Even though you have to look long-term when developing a career plan, progress toward that career is made on a short-term basis. So with that in mind, try to enjoy the journey, and view each small step as positive affirmation that you are headed in the right direction!

Chapter 10

GO BACK TO SCHOOL

Anyone who stops learning is old, whether at 20 or 80. Anyone who keeps learning stays young. The greatest thing in life is to keep your mind young.

Henry Ford

If you are making a career change to an entirely different field, you will need some kind of college degree or technical training. If you have no prior education, consider earning a highly marketable associate degree or a bachelor's degree. If you already have a bachelor's degree, give yourself an employment boost by adding a professional certificate or a graduate degree. Thanks to the availability of distance education options, accelerated programs, and part-time evening or weekend programs, many career changers can obtain more schooling gradually without suffering undue financial hardship.

In most cases, EDUCATION = OPPORTUNITY = MONEY. Education may also be the only way to safeguard yourself against shifting economic conditions. Increasing your work value through education is still one of the best ways to make yourself "recession-proof" in a turbulent economy.

According to the 2008—2018 employment projections from the Bureau of Labor Statistics, occupations that require a college degree are expected to account for nearly half of all new jobs and one-third of all job openings.[1] The typical qualification for 14 of the 30 fastest-growing occupations is a bachelor's degree or higher.[2] These jobs include biomedical engineers, network systems and data communications analysts, financial examiners, medical scientists, physician assistants, biochemists, athletic trainers, computer software engineers, veterinarians, environmental engineers, computer software engineers, survey researchers, physical therapists, and personal financial advisors. Five of the 30 fastest-growing occupations require an associate degree. These jobs include dental hygienists, veterinary technicians, physical therapist assistants, environmental engineering technicians, and occupational therapist assistants. The remaining fastest-growing occupations require some form of job training, usually a year or less. These jobs include home health and personal care aides, skin care specialists, physical therapist assistants, dental assistants, medical assistants, compliance officers, occupational therapist aides, pharmacy technicians, and fitness trainers.

Fastest-growing occupations do not necessarily equate to a large number of jobs so it pays to look at all of the occupational listings provided by the BLS. Registered nursing, for example, ranks fifth (behind cashiers, retail, waiters, and customer service representatives), in occupations with the largest projected number of total job openings due to new job generation and replacement openings.[3] Elementary, secondary, and college teachers, business managers, and accountants and auditors are also good bets as they are projected to add large numbers of jobs in 2008–2018.

John

John was a 29-year-old adult student who used to be in mortgage sales and worked for a broker. He made great money, so he thought he was set and consequently stopped going to school (which he later admitted was stupid). As part of his job, he often called on banks. He began to receive faxes and notices of banks closing, and eventually the industry tanked.

"Now I'm starting all over from scratch," he told me. After he lost his job, he started detailing cars for a living, but that is not what he wants to do for the rest of his life. So he decided to go back to school to finish his degree. He enrolled in a part-time evening program for a networking degree, a strategy that allowed him to keep his job during the day.

THE PROBLEM OF HAVING WORK EXPERIENCE BUT NO DEGREE

I have talked with numerous people who have lots of work experience but no degree. Although they have been very successful with their former companies, the problem is that when they attempt to move to another company to increase their earning potential or want to change their career, they find out they are passed over by younger people with less experience who have degrees. In most cases, there is no recourse except to go back to school to earn their degrees—which is something they do not want to do. What people usually do not realize is that having years of work experience at one company is experience that is too narrowly focused. Thirty years of working at AT&T will not give you the breadth of knowledge that a business degree or MBA will provide. Luckily, colleges are becoming more adult-leaner focused and are offering fast-track or accelerated academic programs and credit for life experience.

Example of a Career Transition to a Related Career

Janine had a master's degree in counseling as well as a nursing degree and was currently working as a nurse in a hospital on third shift. She had a good job, but after so many years of working nights and pulling 12-hour shifts, she felt it was time for a change. Janine said that she "just wanted to be able to spend time with kids, get on that school schedule." After discussing her options, she decided to go back to school to get her school nursing certificate, which she could complete during the day.

THE RELATIONSHIP OF MAJORS TO CAREERS

In today's turbulent economic times, people who attend college are keenly focused on being able to make the best use of their investment by successfully securing employment at graduation. Everyone has heard stories of college students who were unable to find a job in their major, thus adding to the general level of pressure heaped on college students to pick the "right" major. Students, as well as their parents, often mistakenly assume that there should be a direct correlation between major and career. The reality is that not all majors lead to a particular job, and not all jobs require a particular major. It just depends on the requirement established for a particular profession or the set of skills, knowledge, and experience required for a particular job opening. Students in any major can greatly improve their chances of finding employment by knowing how to look for openings and how to market themselves accordingly.

To understand the relationship between major or degree and career or occupation, you must first understand that college majors are organized in terms of broad academic disciplines of majors and minors, whereas the workforce is organized in terms of industries and job functions. To get an idea of how the job market is organized, look at the classified section of your local newspaper. If you read the job descriptions of positions listed under each of these categories, you'll find that each position requires a certain amount of training or education; certification or licensing; skill in a particular area or with a certain piece of equipment; or a specified number of years of experience. The trick is being able to extract the knowledge, skills, and experiences obtained in your major and translate them into the language of the workforce—that is, into skills, degrees, and experience.

In order to have a better grasp of how a major will translate into the world of work, it is important to understand how college majors are organized. In general, college majors are usually housed under a broad academic discipline like Communications, Health Care, Education, or Business. A baccalaureate (four-year) degree in Business, for example, is not just made up of one job but is composed of many different specialty areas, including accounting, actuarial science, economics, finance, information systems, international business, logistics, management, human resources, sales, real estate, and marketing. All these areas, or *majors*, relate to specific job functions in the business world. Majoring in one area allows you to study those specific areas in depth over a period of four years.

Associate (two-year) degrees are generally more career-oriented and are designed to place graduates directly into the workforce in a particular occupation, so there is usually a very clear path between major and job. Examples of such career paths are plumbing and heating technology, electrical engineering technology, registered nursing, culinary arts, veterinary technician, and computer information systems. Now to make things even more confusing, some majors, like Business and Computer Information Systems, have two- and four-year degree options. Two-year degrees offer a sampling of specialty areas (breadth) but not the depth of their four-year counterparts.

Minors are optional complements to a baccalaureate major. A minor typically consists of 18–24 credits in a program outside of a student's major. The purpose of a minor is to provide additional or complimentary knowledge and credentials. Adding a Spanish minor, for example, can make any major much more marketable in today's world. Likewise, a minor in English, Business, or Computer Science provides valuable work-related skills.

Such professional fields as counseling, social work, library science, physical therapy, occupational therapy, and speech pathology have designated the master's degree as the entry-level degree in those professions. Students typically earn a related bachelor's degree, depending on their intended profession, and then continue on to graduate school to earn a master's degree in order to practice. Physicians, chiropractors, veterinarians, lawyers, optometrists, pharmacists, and dentists attend three to four years of study in a professional program beyond the bachelor's degree and then must pass a state licensing exam in order to practice in their respective professions. Anyone interested in teaching at the college or university level will usually need to have completed a master's degree in the subject matter they wish to teach or, preferably, a doctorate in their area of specialization.

But not all college majors lead directly to one job. Some college majors, in particular, four-year liberal arts majors like history, sociology, religious studies, communications, and philosophy, are designed to prepare students for a variety of jobs in the workforce. Liberal arts majors give students a set of skills that can be applied to many different jobs. Graduates possess communication skills, critical thinking skills, the ability to conduct research, and an appreciation for other cultures. Such skills can be used in the business world, at a nonprofit agency, in government, as a customer service supervisor, in sales, or in the admissions or registrar's office of a college or university.

If you look at the help wanted section of your newspaper, you will find there are a number of jobs that require at least a bachelor's degree and some related work experience but do not require a specific major. The jobs include Account Executive, College Administrator, Customer Service Representative, Editorial Assistant, FBI or CIA Special Agent, Fund Raiser, Insurance Agent, Legislative Advocate, Loan Officer, Management Trainee, Manufacturer's Sales Representative, Marketing Research Staff, Police Officer, Private Investigator, Public Relations Worker, Publishing Agent, Educational Sales Consultant, Retail Store Manager, Sales Representative, Travel Agent, Underwriter, and Writer. Students who major in English, Business, Communications, History, Foreign Language, Criminal Justice, Prelaw, Political Science, Mathematics, and Social Sciences can emphasize a particular set of skills and college experiences to qualify for any of the foregoing positions in the workforce. Some students even add a second (or double) major to make themselves more marketable when applying for that first job.

Entrepreneurship is a unique opportunity that may or may not require a particular degree, or it may not require any degree at all. A successful entrepreneur simply needs to have a really good idea and a way to create and sell his or her product or service. Some college majors, like business, lend themselves better than others to helping beginning entrepreneurs understand what's involved in running a business—for example, how to advertise, find a market, distribute your product, or manage the books.

Will I be Successful?

You may wonder if you have what it takes to be successfully in school because your college entrance scores were low or you did not do well in high school. You will be happy to know that the greatest predictor of success in adult students is not your IQ or your high school grades or SAT scores. It is your motivation to complete school and your ability to set a career goal and be willing to work toward achieving it.

Adult students begin school with many doubts: Can I do this? Should I be doing this? Am I neglecting my family? How will I find the time to get everything done? Will my family understand? Will they support me? Am I smart enough to be successful in college? What will the other students in the class think of me? Will I fit in?

Balancing the demands of school, marriage, work, and family responsibilities is critical. Finding enough time to work, study, make the meals, pick up the kids from school activities, and spend quality time with them is critical in making going back to school work. Having a backup babysitting plan is critical in case the babysitter becomes ill.

One adult career-changing student remarked, *"Boy, going back to school after all these years is hard! I had to get used to all the new computer technology. My kids are more computer savvy than I am."*

Back to College (http://www.back2college.com) is an informative site containing a variety of resources for adult students returning to school. Study Skills Self Help Information (http://www.ucc.vt.edu/stdysk/stdyhlp.html) provides an excellent resource of tips and techniques for improving your study skills courtesy of Virginia Tech.

Educational Delivery Options

For students who simply do not have the time to commute to college or attend classes in a traditional classroom format, colleges offer classes in a number of such alternative formats as distance education, online courses, or hybrid options. Some colleges offer fast-track programs that allow students to complete programs in a shorter period of time. Classes are typically held year round but are offered on a shorter cycle than the traditional 15-week semester. Other classes may be held only once a week or on weekends.

Another option designed to shorten the time it takes to complete your degree is receiving college credit for life and work experience. Some colleges accept credits from College-Level Examination Program (CLEP) and Defense Activity for Non-Traditional Education Support (DANTES) examinations or provide a mechanism to evaluate work or life experience through a portfolio review or examination. All these options are subject to a college's particular policies, and there is usually a limit on the number of life experience credits that can be applied to a program.

PAYING FOR SCHOOL

Many companies offer tuition reimbursement benefits for their employees. Some pay all tuition costs, whereas others will pay only a portion of the cost. Check with the human resources department at your place of work to see what tuition reimbursement benefits your company offers.

If you are unemployed and qualify for Trade Act (TRA) benefits or any other type of funding through your local One Stop Career Center, take advantage of that opportunity to train for a new career. Consider going back to school to make yourself more marketable in the event you are not able to find employment in your former career.

Donald

Donald had a BS in English—but he had also taken business courses and had five years' job experience in accounting in a manufacturing firm. Last year, he was laid off because his company closed its operations and relocated to Mexico. Because Donald already has a college degree, he is in a better position than most of his colleagues in the manufacturing plant, who did not have any education beyond high school. With TRA benefits, he now has the opportunity to go back to school, which was something he always wanted to do. Donald debated between finishing an accounting degree and then applying to graduate school to pursue an MBA or teaching English. After doing some research, he found he could finish the requirements for a teaching degree in less time than it would take to complete an MBA. Two and a half years later, he graduated with a teaching certificate and began a position in his new career teaching English at a local high school.

There are many sources of federal, state, and local financial assistance available to career changers. Financial aid is available in three forms: grants and scholarships (which do not have to be repaid), loans (must be repaid), and work-study (campus-based employment). The majority of financial aid is funded by the federal government (examples are the Pell Grant and Stafford Loan Programs), whereas other sources of student aid are funded through your state or your local college or university.

Federal and state grants are usually awarded to the most financially needy applicants, whereas scholarships are usually awarded to individuals who demonstrate academic achievement. Student loans are now available to anyone, regardless of income level, and repayment is usually spread out over a 10-year period of time.

If you do not qualify for financial aid or you still need to borrow more than the federal student loan limits allow, you can elect to borrow an educational loan from a commercial lender. These rates are usually one or two percentage points higher than on federal student loans but are a good alternative if you do not qualify for anything else.

In addition to financial aid, students and their families now have access to several federal tax benefits that help lower college expenses. Examples of such benefits are the Hope Scholarship tax credit and certain allowable deductions for the interest paid on student loans or for tuition payments. Check with your tax accountant for more details.

Applying for financial aid can be confusing and time consuming. Luckily, most states allow students to apply for federal and state financial aid through one application that can be conveniently completed online. This application is called the *Free Application for Federal Student Aid* (FAFSA) and can be found at www.fafsa.ed.gov. The official FAFSA site is a government site, not a dot-com site. If you use a .com site, you will be asked to pay a fee to submit the FAFSA, so use the official government site to submit your application free of charge. *Student Aid on the Web* at www.studentaid.ed.gov is another good source of information about financial aid. There are many good Web sites on the Internet that allow you to search for available scholarships and other sources of funding. All this information is available to the public free of charge through your local college, at your library, or on the Internet.

It is a good idea to have your income tax returns completed before you begin the FAFSA application process, and pay close attention to deadlines. Money is generally distributed on a first-come, first-served basis, so applying early is very important to receive all the money that you are eligible for. The federal government will base your aid eligibility on last year's tax records. If you plan to quit your job or you are now unemployed, your income will be less than what you made last year. Bring this to the attention of the school's financial aid director. The financial aid director is authorized to take special circumstances into account and, where appropriate, may be able to adjust your aid award. If you need help filling out the application or have any questions about the application or awarding process, most colleges and universities have financial aid personnel on staff to answer your questions. College staff will not fill out the application form for you, but they will explain the process and answer any questions you may have.

TEN MAJOR MYTHS ABOUT COLLEGE

Myth 1: I should know what my major is before I start college.

Reality: Most students (up to 80 percent) do not have a clear idea of their career direction when they start college, and many of the ones who do will change their majors for one reason or another. The first two years in college are a great time to explore. It's okay to try something and then decide you want to change direction—its called being "open-minded."

Myth 2: I'll never be able to make it in college because I didn't get good grades in high school.

Reality: Look at the reason why you did not get good grades in high school—was it because of lack of studying? Chances are, those reasons or circumstances no longer exist. The good news is that college is a chance to start fresh. Many students who did not do very well in high school end up excelling in college because they're attending under a different set of circumstances. They are more motivated, more mature, and more serious about their future.

Myth 3: College is just way too expensive.

Reality: In today's uncertain economic times, can you afford *not* to go to college? According to data from the Bureau of Labor Statistics, people with an associate degree earned more than $100 per week more compared to those with a high school diploma.[4] Consider college as an investment in your future. The time and money will be well spent if it allows you to support your family and create the type of life you want.

Myth 4: If I change my major, it will put me behind a whole extra year.

Reality: Not necessarily, for it depends on the major and whether you are a first-year student or a senior. In general, switching majors early in your academic career will result in little or no loss of time, but it will usually take a little longer if you are switching from a non-science-based major to a science-based major than the other way around. But then again, isn't it better (and cheaper) to find out *now* that you do not like a particular major than after you graduate?

Myth 5: If I'm not successful in my very first choice of major, my education will have been wasted.

Reality: This is the "there is one perfect major or career for me out there" myth. The reality is that there are many occupations that have the potential to satisfy your career goals. Once you have clearly defined what you are looking for in a career, you will find that there are a number of paths that match these criteria. A career does not always follow a logical progression, so avoid thinking that only one road will lead you to a satisfying career.

Myth 6: I'll never get a job if I major in art, history, or music.

Reality: The reality is that there are jobs for people in every major—some are just more obvious than others. The trick is to find out what you have to do to make yourself more employable in your particular major and implement those strategies before you graduate. If you stick with what you truly enjoy doing, you will be happier, as well as more successful, in the future.

Myth 7: My major needs to be directly related to the job I'm going to get after I graduate.

Reality: Most college majors are designed to prepare you for a variety of careers. Although professional and technical positions (e.g., Accounting, Education, or Engineering) will often require a specific major, most jobs look for people who possess a set of skills that can be obtained through many different majors.

Myth 8: I don't need to do anything more than get good grades in school to get a good job.

Reality: Good grades help, but in today's competitive job market, you may need more than that. Earning a minor in addition to your major and gaining experience through student organizations, athletics, social groups, student government, internships, summer jobs, and volunteer activities will make you more marketable. Employers consistently place a high value on such experiences.

Myth 9: I know someone who earned a college degree and can't find a job.

Reality: Examine the reasons behind that person's inability to find a job. Then balance your perspective by talking to people who *were* able to find employment in their major. In today's competitive job market, there are only a few occupations that do not require some kind of training or education beyond high school. So a college education, no matter what the major, is a valuable asset.

Myth 10: You have to get a bachelor's degree in order to earn a good living.

Reality: Although a four-year education is never wasted, there are many well-paying occupations, such as Nursing, that require a two-year degree or less. Keep in mind that only 20–25 percent of current jobs require at least a four-year college education. Getting a well-paying job in your chosen occupation depends on many factors, some of which you have no direct control over, such as the economy, the demand in the labor market, or advancements in technology. Today, there are no guarantees, but you can increase your chances of employment with education and experience.

Chapter 11

UPDATE YOUR RESUME AND COVER LETTER

It's not who you are that holds you back, it's who you think you're not.

Author unknown

Unless you have recently changed jobs or applied for something that required a resume, you will probably have to do some major revamping or upgrading to your resume. The best place to start is to dig out an old copy of your resume, dust it off, and if you do not have a copy on a disk, flashdrive, or stored in your computer, start typing or scan in what you already have prepared.

THE PURPOSE OF THE RESUME

The purpose of the resume is to be invited into the interview. Contrary to popular belief, a resume will not get you a job, no matter how good it is. How you perform in the interview is what ultimately determines if you will be offered the position. Employers are looking for employees who can do something for their company (solve a problem, perform a task, manage a department, raise money, sell a product, etc.). To avoid being initially screened out by potential employers, you will need to differentiate yourself from your competition. Therefore, your resume should emphasize the skills and qualities that set you apart from those candidates who have just the baseline qualifications expected in your profession. Then back up those statements with data or bulleted items outlining accomplishments or achievement.

Minimize any potential problems in your work history and maximize your advantages. If you have gaps in your employment, explain how time was spent (went back to school, raised a family, etc.). If you have been with one company for a long time, demonstrate progression within the company by listing each promotion or change in job title as a separate entry.

ELABORATE BUT DO NOT EXAGGERATE

It's true that you want to present your qualities and accomplishments in the best light possible, yet you do not *ever* want to cross the line by misrepresenting yourself. Your age will come out during the interview or background check. The fact that you have exaggerated your skills will become very apparent to an employer and could end up costing you the job one way or the other. I once edited a resume for a young woman who boasted "strong clerical skills, including a wealth of Microsoft Office experience." Sounds great, doesn't it? The problem was that her resume contained text boxes around her headings which made reading her resume very distracting, and her resume was riddled with spelling and grammatical errors. To make things worse, her resume had a .wps extension, which meant it was saved in Microsoft Works (an old software program that came free with many student computers) and could only be opened if the reader had a Microsoft Works converter program. Needless to say, her resume did not back up her claim to having computer and office skills.

Employers check references, require employees to undergo personnel, computer, or basic math and reading skills testing, and in many cases, require applicants to provide a brief demonstration of their computer, teaching, or other skills during the interview process. It's much better to simply say, "I'm sorry, but I'm not that familiar with that software" or "I do not know that software program but I do know ___ and feel sure I could easily pick it up." How effective that admission is depends on how crucial the skill is to the position and whether or not there are other applicants who posses that skill. In any case, lying or exaggerating on your resume or cover letter is never a good idea.

Having said that, however, it is important to highlight or summarize the skills, accomplishments, and abilities that you legitimately possess to an employer. If you are very adept at "resolving customer disputes by phone or in person" but state on your resume that you spent the last five years answering customer service calls, then you are doing yourself, and your skills and experience, an injustice.

WORRIED ABOUT AGE DISCRIMINATION?

Many older career changers are concerned about being viewed as too old or overqualified. Prepare multiple versions of your resume that vary based on the level of the position for which you are applying. Include only past experience that is relevant to the position, and leave out the rest or summarize unrelated work in a single paragraph without dates. Highlight the qualifications you truly hold that would be of benefit in securing the job you want to have.

The second piece of advice is to use a resume format that highlights your experience but deemphasizes your age. Traditional resumes are usually written in a chronological format in which work experience is listed with most current position first. This poses a problem for older workers or those making a career change because the first positions an employer will see on a chronological resume are the jobs from your previous career (which will not help your career change cause.) To highlight your recent career change credentials, use a hybrid resume. This format is slightly different than a functional resume format, which emphasizes skills rather than work chronology. The hybrid format begins with a section that summarizes your career change intentions and transferrable skills or lists your accomplishments at the top of the resume and then places the chronology of work experience toward the bottom of the resume.

TIPS TO AVOID AGE DISCRIMINATION

- Do not provide clues about your age until you are face-to-face.
- List only your last 10 years of experience or those experiences that are directly tied to the position you are seeking. Your early years of experience may no longer be relevant or may not reflect where you want to spend the remainder of your career. Early career history can be lumped into a section titled "previous work history" or "additional experience."
- Only list up-to-date technological or computer skills. It is not necessary to list all the computer software programs you ever learned. List only the current technology being used in the industry today. Having expertise in an outdated manufacturing process or obsolete mainframe computer-programming skills will not help your career change.
- Do not list the dates of your education. In fact, it's illegal for an employer to ask you when you graduated from high school (employers may, however, ask for dates of college graduation).
- To avoid being seen as more expensive than a younger candidate, leave off salary requirements.
- Begin your resume by listing job titles or a summary of your experience to emphasize your value, not your age. Focus on why you are the best person for the job—that's the best way to make age a nonissue.

SHOULD YOU INCLUDE DATES ON YOUR RESUME?

There has been some debate among career professionals regarding the inclusion of dates on a resume. Some resume experts recommend leaving off dates to deemphasize age so the hiring manager will focus on your abilities and skills. Since the purpose of the resume is to be invited to the interview, you certainly do not want to do anything that will give someone with a predisposition to ageism a reason to discard your resume. The downside to not including dates is that it may bring up a red flag to a hiring manager to question the validity of your resume and wonder why the dates were left off. I personally would want to avoid any questions concerning the accuracy of the information provided on my resume. Dates can be deemphasized by placing them in less obvious places and by organizing your resume in a functional format rather than a chronological one. Use the attention-getting left column for job titles, rather than dates. Dates can be discreetly tucked after the company name or placed at the far righthand corner.

Whether or not to include educational and employment dates is a fine issue and sometimes depends on the type of position you are applying for and how much value is placed on educational level. If you recently received a college degree or went back to school to train for a career change, then by all means include the date on your resume to show your recent accomplishment. On the other hand, if you earned your college degree 25 years ago and it's not particularly relevant to the position you are applying for, it is probably okay to leave the date off. The exception would be if your degree is a requirement of the position for which you are applying, such as for faculty or staff positions at a college or university. Bear in mind, however, that the human resources office will go ahead and verify your graduation date anyway, but by then you will perhaps have been called in for an interview and would have had the chance to display your qualifications.

Whether or not you choose to include dates, you want to bring your best qualities to an employer's attention by beginning your resume with a "Career Summary" section or "Professional Profile."

USE A CAREER SUMMARY

Employers spend about 30 seconds on each resume in the first cut. Employers are dealing with volumes of resumes; indeed, some employers receive more than 3,000 resumes a day. If you want your resume to stand out, begin with list of accomplishments, not just job titles. Career changers should use a Career Summary instead of an objective. The problem with an objective is that it is either too general to provide an impact or is too specific. A Career Summary or Professional Profile emphasizes your best accomplishments and still provides the flexibility of targeting your resume to a particular positions or industry.

Two Examples of Well-Written Qualifications Summaries

Example 1

Highly organized and detail-focused **Accounting Professional** with an exceptional track record of accurately handling financial reporting in deadline-oriented environments.

- Fully educated in all aspects of the accounting cycle, reconciling accounts, and ensuring accuracy and completeness of data.
- Excellent computer skills; proficient with Microsoft Word, Microsoft Excel, and QuickBooks and able to learn proprietary systems and applications quickly and easily.
- Knowledge of developing and delivering monthly, quarterly, and annual financial statements.
- Proficiency in managing accounts payable and accounts receivable, generating invoices and monthly statements for clients.

Example 2

Results-driven, PMP®-certified professional with more than 20 years of experience directing and implementing full life cycle of complex, multimillion-dollar programs and initiatives. Proven talent for increasing efficiency, productivity, and product quality through integrated change control and insightful process improvement, consistently delivering projects on time and within budget limitations.

Career summaries address what an employer in the profit sector is interested in: can a potential employee save the company money, make money, solve a specific problem, save time, motivate others to work harder, help the company be more competitive, expand the company's business, get new customers and clients, or keep current customers and clients.

SOFT-SKILL PHRASES TO AVOID OR LIMIT

Many job seekers feel they need to communicate their soft skills, or personal attributes, to the employer to make themselves appear unique. The problem is that so many job seekers claim they have soft skills that most hiring managers pay no attention to them.

The following soft skills are among the most commonly cited:

- Excellent communication skills
- Goal-driven
- Strong work ethic
- Multi-tasker
- Personable presenter
- Goal-oriented
- Detail-oriented

Do not bore your reader with such overused and tired phrases as shown in the foregoing list. It is much more effective to write descriptions that are action-based and demonstrate your abilities rather than just laying claim to them. For example, rather than just stating you are an "excellent presenter," you could say something like "Developed and presented 45 multi-media presentations to new clients resulting in 30 new accounts totaling $300,000 in new revenues."

MODERNIZE YOUR RESUME

Resume formats and methods of delivery have dramatically changed over the years. If you have been out of the job market for a while, you may be surprised to see how much has changed. If you have a blog or a Web site, or e-portfolio, list the URL on your resume.

- *Old Rule:* **Use colored or textured paper.**
  New Rule: **Use plain white paper.** In the past, applicants would purchase expensive classic laid or linen colored paper to make their resume stand out in a crowd. With more jobs applicants applying online or by e-mail or fax, it is perfectly acceptable to use standard white 8 × 11 paper.
- *Old Rule:* **Place keywords in a separate section at the top of the resume.**
  New Rule: **Integrate keywords into the entire document.**
- *Old Rule:* **Use an "Objective."**
  New Rule: **Use a "Summary of Qualifications" or "Profile."** Objectives are either too general to be of any use or are too specific and must be modified for each position you apply for.

- *Old Rule:* **Describe job duties in the passive voice.**
  New Rule: **Use action verbs rather than passive descriptors.** Phrases indicative of the passive voice include "responsible for," "duties included," "served as." Rather than saying, "Responsible for the supervision of three sales staff," change your description to "Supervised three sales staff." The result is a shorter, more direct mode of writing that adds impact to the way the resume reads.
- *Old Rule:* **Never abbreviate anything on a resume or cover letter.**
  New Rule: **Abbreviating is fine, as long as it is understandable.** This is the age of texting and Twitter, where everything is abbreviated, condensed, and minimized. It's fine to write "St." instead of "Street." However, acronyms should still be spelled out the first time they're mentioned. For example: Total Quality Management (TQM).
- *Old Rule:* **List your job responsibilities for each job under such a heading as "Duties Included."**
  New Rule: **Use bullet points.** You'll waste a lot of resume space if you write "Duties Included" on a separate line after every job. Just summarize your main accomplishments and qualifications in bullet points, and start each bullet point with an action verb in past tense (Supervised, Managed, Streamlined, Coordinated, Prepared, etc.).
- *Old Rule:* **Provide a reason for leaving each position.**
  New Rule: **It is not necessary to give a reason for leaving each job.** Prepare an answer in your mind for the interview if the subject should come up, but it is not necessary to indicate a reason in the resume or cover letter. However, do plan and practice a response in case the question comes up in an interview. Make your answer a brief, factual statement and do not complain about your former boss or position.
- *Old Rule:* **Include vital statistics.**
  New Rule: **Leave off personal information (weight, height, marital status, health status, number of children).** Such information could be used to influence a hiring decision, although doing so remains illegal.
- *Old Rule:* **Include personal interests.**
  New Rule: **Do not include hobbies or interests.** Job hunters used to include hobbies on a resume to indicate well-roundedness. Unrelated hobbies and interests are irrelevant to the position and may actually act as a deterrent to your work-related skills and abilities.
- *Old Rule:* **List the complete address and name of supervisor of each position.**
  New Rule: **Do not list addresses of previous employers or professional associations.** Providing such data is no longer necessary.
- *Old Rule:* **List your references on your resume.**
  New Rule: **Do not include references in your resume.** References take up valuable space. It is more appropriate to list references on a separate sheet of paper.

- *Old Rule:* Finish your resume with "References available upon request."

  New Rule: **A reference statement is no longer necessary.** It is assumed that you will provide whatever additional information the employer requests. Instead of including a reference statement on your resume, prepare a list of three to five references on a separate sheet that you can give to an employer.

- *Old Rule:* **Limit your resume to one page.**

  New Approach: **It is acceptable to extend the resume to two pages if you have extensive skills, experience, publications, or other accomplishment.** However, keeping a resume to one page is a good rule of thumb for new graduates who have little or no work experience.

- *Old Rule:* **You should show every job you have ever held and give each equal importance.**

  New Rule: **Your employment history should only go back as far as it is related to your current employment objectives.** Think of your resume as a marketing piece that highlights the best parts of your collective work and educational experience rather than as a memoir.

- *Old Rule:* **Your resume should go back no more than 10 or 15 years.**

  New Rule: **Do not use an arbitrary number to determine how much to include on your resume.** Use the rule of relevancy to decide how *many* of your jobs to include.

- *Old Rule:* **One resume should handle everything.**

  New Rule: **Not anymore!** Tailor your resume for every job you apply for because each job has unique requirements. Writing different versions of your resume does not mean you should falsify your experience or misrepresent yourself; it does mean, however, that you should highlight and focus the skills and experience you have that are relevant to that job. Today, it is a good idea to have a traditional Word format and a plain-text format of your resume to accommodate the different types of employment application procedures.

Normally, I do not advise listing interests and hobbies, except for community activities; but in the case of a career changer, this section can be advantageous. By saying that you engage in volleyball tournaments or teach aerobics, you imply that you are physically fit and healthy—something an employer would like to ask but cannot. By listing an interest in genealogy, you imply research abilities. The purpose of listing specific hobbies is to present yourself as an interesting, well-rounded person. Who knows, you may just be able to connect with an employer who's also an avid stamp-collecting enthusiast and get the job.

Lastly, carefully consider your word choice. The resume is your introduction to the employer. He or she will be formulating a first impression of your skills and abilities. Advertising and marketing companies put careful thought and consideration into each and every word that goes into marketing copy, and you should do the same in your resume. The words you use on your resume represent you to the recruiter when you cannot be there to speak for yourself, so they need to showcase you in a powerful way.

COMMON RESUME MISTAKES

- **Spelling and grammar mistakes.** Do not solely rely on *Spell Check* because it will not pick up contextual errors. The need for checking and proofreading cannot be stressed enough. With so many resumes out there for one position, typos are a guaranteed death sentence. Also remember that you are creating an impression. Therefore, you want that first impression to be professional. If your resume is sloppy, a recruiter or hiring manager may wonder, or even assume, that you are equally sloppy in your professional work.
- **Listing high school education.** If you have some college or technical education beyond high school, do list this. It is not necessary to list your high school education—this will date you. High school graduation or a GED is implied if have a college education.
- **Job descriptions too long or not results-oriented.** Be brief and concise, and make each word count. You do not have to list everything. Use action verbs that show the higher-level job duties held—*supervised, developed, coordinated,* or *managed,* for example, rather than lower-level responsibility job tasks like *filed, counted,* or *waited on customers.*

Prepare two copies of your resume: a standard Word format for printouts or responding to ads in classifieds, and a plain-text version, also known as a *scannable resume,* that includes keywords to use for online applications. In today's high-tech corporate climate, the bigger companies, and even the smaller ones, will scan resumes into an applicant tracking system or a searchable database for future retrieval. To accommodate such systems, the resume will need to be stripped of some of its "bells and whistles" to eliminate such decorative elements as horizontal or vertical lines and fancy fonts. A simple nonserif format like Arial or Times Roman works best. List keywords separated by commas or periods. Keywords are such nouns that reflect your experience as your job title (e.g., Systems Analyst or Account Executive), industry expertise (e.g., Microsoft Excel, TCP/IP, C++), or education (e.g., Master's of Business Administration, BS in Engineering). A keyword summary is ideally placed just before the Professional Experience section of your resume.

If you send your resume to an employer by e-mail, always put something in the subject line to indicate the purpose of your e-mail and begin the e-mail by introducing yourself and the fact that you are attaching your resume in consideration of the position you are applying for (just as you would in a cover letter). Such steps help eliminate the problem of your e-mail being identified as SPAM and will entice the employer to open your e-mail. If you have years of transferrable experience, you can use the subject line to your advantage by writing, "Experienced Sales Professional for Account Management Position." Depending on the job you are applying for, some employers will not accept e-mail attachments; others will accept only a PDF file or a Word attachment. Always follow the instructions for submitting a resume for a job opening.

CAREER CHANGE LANGUAGE

The following examples illustrate career change language that can be used when making the transition from an old career to a new career.

Seeking to use 15 years of experience in the manufacturing industry to obtain a position maintaining and repairing Plumbing, Heating, and Air Conditioning systems.

Applying my knowledge of neonatal nursing procedures and my passion for quality patient care to the educational field as a clinical supervisor.

Utilizing my ten years of successful experience in education to transition into educational sales.

THE COVER LETTER

Many employers still like to see some kind of a cover letter, however brief, even if you e-mail your resume. Today, the cover letter does not need to be sent as a separate document unless you are sending the resume through regular mail. If you are sending your resume by e-mail or fax, the cover letter is simply the e-mail message that accompanies the attached resume. Because today's attention span is much shorter than it was 20 years ago, the cover letter is going to focus on qualifications and the resume is going to focus on accomplishments. Since many recruiters are using the introductory e-mails as screening tools to decide whether or not to open a resume, match the qualifications listed in your e-mail as closely as possible to the working of the requirements specified in the job description.

Whether sending an e-mail or paper cover letter, try not to send a generic cover letter that begins with the salutation "To Whom It May Concern." Find out the name of the person to whom you must send the letter by doing a little research ahead of time. Look up the name of the hiring manager on the company's Web site or call the company for the appropriate name. Hiring managers and recruiters are looking for employees that fit their needs, not someone who is blindly sending out resumes to any old job opening.

Just because you are sending an e-mail does not mean you should not use standard cover letter protocol. Check your spelling and grammar, write in a professional style, and avoid text-messaging language and cute emoticons. Lastly, send the e-mail to yourself to make sure the formatting works and the letter is ready to send.

A sample e-mail cover letter and a traditional cover letter format are included in the Appendix.

Chapter 12

ARE YOU READY TO BEGIN YOUR CAREER CHANGE?

How you respond to the challenge in the second half will determine what you become after the game, whether you are a winner or a loser.

Lou Holtz

I recently watched a documentary on Animal Planet about an elk population living near a city in Canada. The only reason they were able to be successful and thrive is because they learned to adapt to their changing habitat and found a way to coexist with humans. It struck me that this story was similar to the one faced by many Americans who worked in a manufacturing plant for most of their lives only to find themselves out of a job because the plant went out of business or moved its operations to Mexico. Most recently, Wall Street financial professionals found themselves in a similar situation and were uprooted from the comfort of their lucrative jobs and lifestyles.

In our turbulent economic times, it's all about being flexible and adapting to changing times and surroundings. Jobs come and go, new technologies develop, and new occupations emerge. If you are caught unawares, you may become stretched past your comfort zone. Today, it is necessary to constantly retool, reinvest, and continually upgrade to give yourself more options when change does occur.

Are you prepared to make your career change?

- Do you understand what is involved in changing your career?
- Do you know what to do to upgrade your skills?
- Have you updated your resume?
- Do you understand the salary implications in changing your career?
- Have you checked your appearance or updated your interviewing wardrobe?
- Are you psychologically prepared to go through the job search process?

THE CONCEPT OF MENTAL TOUGHNESS

A successful job search starts and ends with a positive attitude. To remain positive during your job search and to search and interview for jobs confidently without giving up takes some emotional fortitude. Sports announcers and coaches frequently talk about the concept of mental toughness. Think about the quarterback who fumbles the ball or throws an interception in a critical down of a play. The worst thing he can do is get flustered and throw another interception. The best thing he can do is forget about it, pick up the ball, and go out there and throw a touchdown. Learning to forget about a bad play and move on to the next play is an attitude that helps football players win games and would go a long way to helping job seekers progress from one job interview to the next.

A key component of mental toughness is being able to think confidently and overcome frustration or negativity.[1] Some of the other characteristics of mental toughness that can be applied to the process of looking for a job are listed here:

- *Self-Belief.* Confidence in yourself and your abilities. The belief in your ability to be successful in your job search.
- *Motivation.* The ability to keep plugging away, continue studying, attending school, working toward your career goal while working and taking care of your family. To continue to apply for jobs and go through interviews until you are offered a job even though times are tough and you experience rejection.
- *Focus.* The ability to maintain focus on what you need to do to get a job. To remember the points you want to make during an interview and be able to focus on answering the questions, despite being nervous. To not be distracted from the task at hand by what others do or say or by your own internal worry or negative self-talk. Focus comes with the practice of interviewing and talking about yourself to potential employers.
- *Composure.* The ability to keep your calm during a stressful situation. Being able to handling pressure and to bounce back after a setback.

Think about how difficult it is to deal with rejection from a potential employer without becoming discouraged and the frustration of waiting for a response to an application, a post-job interview decision, or an e-mail or phone inquiry about the status of an opening. Too many job seekers give up prematurely or unintentionally sabotage their chances by becoming discouraged, feeling pessimistic, or losing confidence. The ability to remain composed during an interview despite feeling nervous, especially when asked difficult interview questions, can often make the difference between you or another candidate winning the position.

THE WAITING GAME

Today's job seekers have to be able to tolerate the frustration of waiting when looking for a job. All job seekers would like to get a job as soon as possible so they can begin their new careers. Unfortunately, sometimes it just does not work that way. In today's world of online applications, it is very common not to receive an acknowledgment of your job application or a confirmation that the organization to whom you sent your resume received it. This lack of response is the frustrating reality of applying to companies that only accept online applications.

While the job seeker is waiting for a response, the employer may simply be swamped with hundreds of applications for a single opening and may not have the time or resources to respond to every applicant. Then, when the employer does call or e-mail, the job seeker is often caught unaware.

For some candidates, the only time they know the process is complete is when they get a letter in the mail telling them they were not selected for the opening. Some companies never send a letter, though. Many companies will wait until the selected candidate has actually accepted the position before informing the other candidates that they were not selected. Only when the selected candidate does not accept an offer do they call the next person on the list. In the meantime, candidates are waiting and wondering what went wrong. Many hiring managers have had to scale back on filling positions because of budget shortfalls, and those that are left may be as efficient in managing their time or responding to phone or e-mail inquiries as you would like. All these reasons are factors, and events that go on behind the scenes have absolutely nothing to do with you. Most of the time, the delay is because a last-minute candidate appeared on the scene who was exactly what the employer was looking for, or the company decided to eliminate the position, or because the hiring process was put on hold because of budgetary considerations.

How can job seekers minimize uncertainly and exercise a degree of control over their situation? By understanding that their timeline is not the same as the employer's timeline. As a job seeker, you need to gain as much information as you can by diligently following up on the status of your application or interview every two weeks by phone or e-mail, because some information is better than no information. Most importantly, do not feel that you have to wait helplessly by the phone. Continue to actively search for openings, apply for jobs, and participate in interviews.

MAINTAINING COMPOSURE

The best way to keep your composure during an interview or any other stressful) situation is to prepare yourself ahead of time. Practice calming yourself through relaxation, deep breathing techniques, or meditation. Periodically program your mind for success with positive affirmations and expectations.[2] Building mental job toughness is like building muscle: you have to work at it in order to make it stronger.

Another trick to maintaining composure is learning to let go of mistakes quickly. Letting go allows you to refocus on what you need to do to answer the next question confidently. If you have a bad interview, get stuck on a question, or become confused, take a deep breath to regain your composure and ask for clarification if needed. Then, answer the question as best you can, forget it, and focus on the next question. After the interview, step back and learn what you can from the experience and continue looking. If you do not get the job, take a moment to acknowledge whatever disappointment, anger, or frustration you are feeling, then move past it. Again, learn whatever you can from the experience to improve your skills and continue on to the next job opportunity.

DEALING WITH REJECTION

Job seekers have to be psychologically prepared to deal with the possibility of rejection. You may not be selected to participate in an interview, or you may receive a letter telling you that another "more qualified" candidate was selected. It's difficult to maintain a positive attitude in the face of rejection, but you need to put it into a more positive framework. Avoid taking rejection personally or thinking that someone else "took" that job away from you. The other candidate may have had more years of experience or was a better fit with the company. That's just part of the job search process.

Do not sabotage your chances for obtaining a new career by becoming overly frustrated or developing a negative attitude that will spill over to the way you interact with potential employers. Stay positive and focused. To help keep up your spirits, surround yourself with people who are encouraging; also read motivational sayings, or do whatever helps to stay positive. If you begin to feel discouraged or down, take a break; go out to do something enjoyable. Continuing to look forward and focus on what you want to occur, rather than thinking about the things that can go wrong. The more jobs you apply for, the more people you talk to, the more interviews you attend, the greater your chances are that at least one of them will result in a job offer. Do not feel too bad about missing a job offer with one company because something better may be just around the corner.

TAKING CONTROL OF YOUR JOB SEARCH

To feel better about yourself and your job search, it helps to understand there are parts of the job search process that you can control and parts that you have no control over. For example, you have no control over who else applies for the position. In some cases, you may be the best candidate for the position; but in other situations, you may be up against others who have more experience. Although you can dramatically increase or decrease the chances of being hired for a position by the way you present yourself in the interview, you ultimately have no control over who an employer hires. The worst thing tired and frustrated job seekers can do is to adopt the view that employers are out to get them and that the job search process is out of their control. Employers do need people to fill their positions, but sometimes who an employer selects has more to do with internal factors than with your qualifications. Realizing that point helps you view the process more objectively and decreases the likelihood that you will take the rejection personally.

DO NOT JEOPARDIZE YOUR CURRENT SITUATION

If you are currently still employed, avoid jeopardizing your current position by using the company fax, printer, or e-mail to send out or print resumes. Employers can monitor your e-mail, and using work time to scope out another position, or even to study while attending school at night, will be considered an abuse of company time and resources. Use your lunch hour or take vacation or sick days to search for a job. If you work in a casual work environment, be mindful that showing up in a suit may cause attention. Bring a change of clothes with you and change in a restroom. When applying for jobs, you may want to avoid blind advertisements or ones where the name of the company is not specified, since the ad could be from your current employer. Online job boards do give you the ability to block certain companies from viewing your resume. Common sense and courtesy will smooth the transition.

Whatever you do, do not give up. It may take longer than you like to find a new job, but there are interested employers and positions waiting for you.

Chapter 13

WHERE TO FIND
JOB OPENINGS

*Perseverance is a great element of success. If you only knock long enough and loud
enough at the gate, you are sure to wake up something or somebody.*

Henry Wadsworth Longfellow

Now that you are ready to begin looking for a job in your new career, where do
you begin? If it has been some time since you have had to look for a job, you
may find that things have changed considerably. The traditional method of sending a resume by mail has been replaced by e-mail attachments and online job
boards. Although many jobs are still advertised in the classified ads section of your
local newspaper, classified ads can now be viewed on the Internet, and employers
are increasingly relying on posting their job openings on their company Web sites,
through computer kiosks, on online job boards, and through staffing agencies and
plain old word-of-mouth referrals. If you attend a job fair, recruiters may ask you
to apply online through their company Web site or by means of a kiosk located
in one of their stores instead of handing you a paper application.

SEARCH TACTICS

Many career strategists have said that searching for a job *is* a full-time job. This
cannot be emphasized enough, especially in a tight job market. The key to a successful job search is being organized, remaining diligent, and devoting a block of
time each day to searching for and following up on job leads. Use the same professionalism, discipline, and ingenuity to finding a new job that you demonstrated during your first career. Your job search should be thorough and systematic. When
contacting employers, conduct yourself in a professional manner at all times. Write
in complete sentences when corresponding by e-mail, and review your e-mail
address and voicemail messages to see if they convey the kind of message you want
to send a potential employer.

Begin your job search by laying out an overall strategy. Will you be looking locally,
regionally, or nationally for a job? Where will you look for job openings? Create a log
or spreadsheet of companies in your chosen field to help you target your job search
activities. Keep track of your progress by listing and updating your leads, contacts,
action taken, and the status of your applications.

WHERE TO FIND JOB OPENINGS

According to data from the Bureau of Labor Statistics, the most popular method of finding work for unemployed workers 20–64 years of age has been to contact employers directly, followed by sending out resumes and filling out job applications, using friends or relatives for contacts, utilizing public employment agencies, answering ads, using an "other" source, and using a private employment agency. Whereas 20- to 34-year-olds used one to two job search methods, 35- to 64-year-olds commonly used two methods.[1]

After giving Linda, an unemployed marketing professional, some job lead suggestions, I apologized because I was not sure the so-called leads would actually lead to anything. Linda said she would follow up on any lead because "it just might that 'what the heck' try that leads to something." Linda described herself as being more effective talking to people face-to-face, a method better than just sitting back and sending out resumes or talking my e-mail. She provided some good advice. If someone does not like what you have (or do not have) on your resume, you may be eliminated before you have a chance to discuss it with them and show your strengths.

To gain a competitive advantage over younger applicants, do not rely solely on your resume—get out there and knock on doors or use the telephone or e-mail or computer to seek out openings. Use your face-to-face communications skills to talk to human resources people about possible job openings. Utilize the hundreds of people you have worked with over the years who know your skills and experience to help identify job openings or leads. Use your contacts to discover background information about a company so you can use that information to your benefit to become a more attractive candidate to an employer.

Too many people miss out on possible job opportunities because they make assumptions about a position without gathering the facts. They assume that the job is not something they would want or that the employer will not be interested in them. Avoid making such assumptions. Instead, apply for every job you think you might be qualified for.

Begin by identifying possible employment candidates by searching telephone directories, business directories, or computer databases, which are available in most public libraries. Then, narrow your list down and e-mail or make telephone calls to the human resources office of each potential employer. If you will be looking for employment in another city or state, check the yellow pages online at www.yellowpages.com, www.superpages.com, or http://yp.yahoo.com, or www. Hoovers.com.

To increase the chances of successfully finding a job, use multiple resources rather than just the Internet or the Sunday newspaper to find openings. If you are looking for a job in a market that has many openings, you may need to use only one source to find employment. However, if you live in an economically depressed area where there have been many layoffs, you will probably have to use all the resources at your disposal to find a job. Do not forget to check trade journals, examine occupation-specific Web sites, or even visit an executive recruiter or staffing agency.

Here are a few other places to find job leads:

- Public employment services such as your One Stop Career Center, Workforce Development Center, local chamber of commerce, and community job-posting sites.
- Internet job boards, job search engines, company Web sites, and Web sites for specific industries or professional organizations.
- College or university career offices and alumni organizations.
- Women's centers and community-based career services for people who belong to a particular "special population" category, such as single parents, displaced homemakers, or members of an underrepresented group based on gender or ethnicity.
- Trade magazine or journal and professional organization Web sites' career sections, former sorority or fraternity organizations or special interest or alumni associations, and industry- or occupation-specific Internet sites and job boards.
- Job or career fairs in your local or regional area.
- Executive recruiters or employment agencies (also called staffing or personnel agencies). When using such agencies, find out whether they charge you, or the employer, a fee for their services.

NETWORKING

You tell a friend, who tells his (or her) friend, who talks to a neighbor who just had a meeting with his (or her) boss about hiring another manager. With this information, you have just discovered a job opening you may never have known about. This process is networking. Reaching out to friends, neighbors, acquaintances, former employers, professors, and community members allows you, through the people *they* know, to connect with more people than you could possibly reach by yourself.

A recent survey by Bankrate validates an old truism: It is often not *what* you know, but *who* you know. Thirty-three percent of employed workers said that they found their current position through networking, and another 14 percent volunteered that they had found it through friends or family, which also counts as networking.[2]

As someone who has been in the workforce for a number of years, you have a vast number of resources you may be unaware of or may have forgotten about. Make a list of all the people you have worked with over the years, including

- Professional acquaintances and associates
- Former employers
- Former coworkers

- Old business contacts
- Past customers or clients
- Former or current members in professional associations

Also include friends, neighbors, classmates, former teachers, people at your church or synagogue, your beautician or barber, your doctor, your banker, your attorney, or anyone else you have known over the years who may be able to provide you with some helpful job leads.

Use common sense when networking. You do not have to talk to 100 strangers a day or be pushy or appear desperate. Simply select a few individuals and ask for their help or any information they have about jobs or people you might contact. As a courtesy, be conscious of the other person's time, and respect the limits to which that person is willing to help you. Do your research ahead of time to be able to select your networking contacts judiciously and make maximum use of their expertise and advice. Do not waste you or your contact's time by asking simple questions you could answer with some basic research. Always ask permission to use your contact's name when approaching another contact, and be sure to thank the person for the information he or she has provided you with.

If you feel embarrassed about admitting that you need help finding a job or are hesitant to approach strangers, then begin with people you know and feel comfortable talking with. Take on the role of an "information seeker." The quality of your networking contacts, not the quantity, may actually be more helpful to you in the end. People are more willing to recommend someone they know than someone they have only met casually.

Facebook and LinkedIn are social networking sites that have taken networking to the next level. They will be discussed in more detail in Chapter 14.

Keep a Contact Log

Establish a progress log to keep track of the ads to which you have responded so that you do not answer the same ad twice (see Table 13.1). Keep a record of the companies to which you have submitted applications or resumes. Unless the ad specifically tells you not to respond with a phone call, follow up on each submission with a phone call after two weeks. When you call, simply tell the employer that you are checking on the status of your application and that you would like to schedule an interview. Sometimes, this simple three-minute call can make all the difference in your job search. Employers will respect your determination, especially in the sales and marketing professions, where perseverance is a key quality in a successful employee.

Hiring is also industry-dependent. In some industries, job openings are always advertised in the paper; whereas others are advertised by word of mouth. Companies like automotive shops, retail shops, or restaurants will commonly hang a sign outside the shop advertising their opening.

If you are a career changer who will be graduating from college, apply early. People mistakenly believe they need to wait until they graduate to apply for a job opening. In

Table 13.1
Sample Job Search Log

Date	Action	Contact	Position	Notes
Company Name: ABC Corp.				
6/1/2009	Called	Mr. Jones 675-9124	Sales Manager	Talked to Mr. Jones. Suggested I apply in 2 weeks for opening.
6/15/2009	Filled out application		Sales Associate	
Company Name: Toft				
6/1/2009	E-mailed resume	Human Resources	Accounts Mgr.	
6/12/2009	Received phone call	Mr. Smith	Accounts Mgr.	Scheduled interview on 6/15/09

the nursing field, hiring is often done as early as January. Apply for job placement services with your college career center and attend all job fairs and on-campus interviews. I advise my students to start attending job fairs in their freshman year so they can practice their 30-second elevator pitch and begin making contacts.

Free Job Search Engines

Career Builder	www.careerbuilder.com
Craigslist	www.craigslist.com
FlipDog	www.flipdog.monster.com
Glassdoor	www.glassdoor.com
HotJobs	www.hotjobs.yahoo.com
Indeed	www.indeed.com
Job Web	www.jobweb.com
JobBank USA	www.jobbankusa.com
Jobster	www.jobster.com
LinkUp	www.linkup.com
Monster	www.monster.com
SimplyHired	www.simplyhired.com
True Careers	www.truecareers.com
Yahoo!HotJobs	www.yahoo.com

Free Career-Specific Job Search Web Sites

Academic	www.apnjobs.com, http://chronicle.com/jobs/, http://higheredjobs.com/
Accountants	www.financialjobs.com
Agriculture	www.usda.gov
Automotive	www.autojobs.com
CareerOneStop	www.careeronestop.org
Chamber of Commerce	www.chamberofcommerce.com
Civil Service Commission	www.scsc.state.pa.us
Computer/IT	www.dice.com
Construction	www.constructionjobs.com
Education	www.teachers-teachers.com
Employment Guide	www.employmentguide.com
Engineering	www.engineeringjobs.com
Environment	http://tomah.com, www.environmental-jobs.com, www.ecojobs.com
Federal Jobs	www.usajobs.opm.gov
Food Service	www.foodservice.com
Government	www.govtjobs.com
Green Jobs	www.sustainlane.com
Health Care	www.healthcaresource.com
Hospitality	www.hcareers.com
Human Services	www.therapyjobzone.com
HVAC	www.hvacagent.com
Journalism	www.journalismjobs.com
Landscape/Engineering	www.e-architect.com, http://aecjobbank.com
Law Enforcement	www.911hotjobs.com, www.officer.com
Lawyers	www.alternativelawyerjobs.com
Outdoor	www.coolworks.com
Part-Time	www.snagajob.com
Physicians	www.healthsearchusa.com
Plumbing	www.plumbingagent.com
Public Administration	www.opajobs.com
Science	www.scienceonline.org, www.onassignment.com
Social Work	www.socialworker.com
Technology	www.brassring.com, www.cramsession.com
Theater/Dance	http://www.tcg.org

Chapter 14

How to Utilize the Latest Technology

The Internet is just a world passing around notes in a classroom.

Jon Stewart

Using the Internet in Your Job Search

You can use the Internet as a way to search for jobs that would otherwise be difficult to locate. Just a mere 10 years ago, job seekers used to blindly mail out a batch of resumes to prospective companies. That method used costly stamps, and sitting around waiting for a response wasted a lot of a job seeker's time. Internet searching is quicker, easier, and less costly. Job seekers can search for job openings in any part of the country; they can research companies, compare wages, calculate relocation costs, review state employment trends, post a resume, or network, all from the comfort of their homes or local Internet cafes.

Begin your job search by visiting such large Internet employment sites as CareerBuilder.com or Monster.com. The sheer number of listings will give you an idea of what openings are available in the marketplace. Then, narrow your search by using smaller search engines, recruiter sites, and individual company Web sites.

Such search engines as Google (www.google.com) or Yahoo (www.yahoo.com) allow you to find information on the Web using key words and phrases. There are also such mega search engines as Dogpile (www.dogpile.com) that search using several engines at once.

Job search engines allow you to search for openings and post your resume, and some even provide resume, job search, and other career-related advice and information. There are many good job search engines available; you may want to use several to get the most results. An example of a career-specific or "niche" job search engine is Dice (www.dice.com), which is a recommended site for IT jobs.

Online job boards are most useful to people who have a particular profession, skill, or area of expertise in a niche market that can be targeted through an online job board. Job boards are of less value to job seekers who have a general set of skills or a varied employment history. To make the most use of job boards, career changers need to be careful in selecting or emphasizing skills on their resume that will directly apply to a new job. Limit your list of previous, unrelated duties, since applicant-searching software will pick up those keywords as well.

SENDING A RESUME BY E-MAIL

When applying by e-mail, you can write your cover letter in the body of the e-mail or attach it as a separate document. But when sending a resume by e-mail, always attach it to the e-mail. Do not cut and paste your resume into the body of the e-mail because the formatting may be rearranged during the transmission process.

Include your name and the position you are applying for in the subject line of the e-mail. If you are sending a resume without a cover letter, always include a brief introductory statement of why you are writing. Human resources staff receive hundreds of e-mails each day. Do not assume they will automatically know why you are sending them your resume. And lastly, but just as important, do not forget to include your contact information either in the cover letter or as a signature line at the bottom of your e-mail so the employer can easily contact you.

APPLYING ONLINE

Today, many companies accept resumes and applications only online. Applying online is very simple. You will be asked to upload your resume (use a plain-text format) or will be given directions to fill in a form or application. Be sure to follow all the directions exactly.

Some search engines, like CareerBuilder, will ask you to select your skills from a prescribed list. Remember to select those skills that are relevant to your future job, not those that apply only to your past job or career. If you are asked to list work experience or job positions, first list work experience relevant to your new career, then list work experience that relates to your previous career, or simply do not include previous work experience at all if it occurred more than 10 years ago.

Finally, do not use a work e-mail account when applying to jobs online or when sending out a resume by e-mail. Set up a separate e-mail account dedicated for job searching or use your home account. Employers are capable of monitoring your e-mail at work and will consider your using work time to apply for another position an unauthorized use of company property.

SOCIAL NETWORKING SITES

Such social networking sites as MySpace, Facebook, and LinkedIn have gained enormous popularity in recent years. These sites are not only a way to keep in touch with friends but also a way to network with other professionals, connect with potential employers, and learn about possible job openings. Facebook is very useful for connecting with old friends, whereas LinkedIn is designed for those people who want to create a professional brand and build and expand their professional network. LinkedIn provides a greater degree of privacy than Facebook or MySpace. In LinkedIn, people can only be connected through an introduction. Who can you connect with? Undergraduate and graduate students, people in academia, business owners, professionals, and entrepreneurs are all possible contacts through LinkedIn. If you are a college graduate, you can use LinkedIn to connect to alumni (potential mentors) in your future career. Sometimes we feel hesitant to "bother" people we do not know. But LinkedIn is exactly the place to make such connections because its members have opted into this group, which exists solely for the purpose of networking. LinkedIn will also let you research company profiles, connect with employees, and even view their career paths. The last valuable source of information that you can get from using LinkedIn is human resources contacts. Look on "popular profiles," which will often list human resources personnel because they are the most commonly searched contacts in a company.

Recruiters are now using MySpace, Facebook, and LinkedIn to search for candidates. If you have not joined LinkedIn, consider doing so. It's free, and with a little investment of your time, you can build a useful professional network that can find you your next position. A LinkedIn profile is also a great way to show potential employers that you are up to speed with the latest networking technology. Take as much care creating a professional, credible, and impressive profile as you did your resume. Once your profile is complete, you can create a LinkedIn URL address that can be attached to the signature line of your e-mail or listed in a resume. Remember to keep your profile up-to-date and check it at least once a week. Add your Facebook or LinkedIn link to the bottom of your e-mail signature. It is then very easy to forward your link to others.

OTHER NETWORKING TOOLS

Instant messaging (IM) can help you with your job search because it is another way to network.[1] Use a professional screen name and write brief, concise messages using full sentences.

Twitter is a free social networking and micro-blogging service that enables its users to send and read messages known as *tweets*. Tweets are text-based posts of up to 140 characters. Twitter can be used to poke around for a job, follow companies, or create a job search network. Just for fun, try a short "self-advertisement" on twitter and see what kind of response you receive!

Many career services offices now offer services through e-mail, IM, Facebook, LinkedIn, and Twitter; so if you are a career changer who is about to graduate or have recently graduated, you may be able to receive job search support by means of these tools. As the popularity of social networking sites grows, more and more companies, career coaches, and employment recruiters will use these tools to reach customers and potential employees in the future.

VIDEO RESUMES

Video resumes are the latest craze to hit the job market. But are they really a good idea? A well-made video resume can help you be noticed and stand out among the dozens of people vying for the same job, but a poorly done video can seriously damage your chances of ever getting an interview.

Many employers do not have the time to watch a video resume or are worried about opening themselves up to a discrimination suit. So it will pay to know the "hiring culture" of your particular career field to determine whether sending a video resume is even acceptable.

If you are going to do a video resume, make sure your video resume is brief (one to three minutes), professional, polished, and perfect before you send it to a potential employer. Write a script before you begin recording, and make sure you produce it in a location that is free from distractions. Dress professionally and look directly into the video camera. Begin the video by introducing yourself, then give a brief description of your interests, skills, and work experience. You may want to take several practice videos before sending your finished video resume out to an employer. Once you have a video resume you are satisfied with, you can list it on your resume; post it online; add a link to your blog, Facebook, or LinkedIn profile; or upload it to YouTube or to a job search site like CareerBuilder or Jobster.

DISTANCE INTERVIEWING TECHNOLOGY

Distance interviewing technology has been around for some time. Colleges use this technology to "beam" classes to students at off-campus locations. Businesses use conferencing technology to conduct meetings with employees at sister or parent companies in other locations or to negotiate business deals with potential customers or clients at locations across the United States or overseas. Using this technology avoids the time and expense of travel.

Employers use distance interviewing technology to interview candidates who are geographically dispersed across the company, thereby saving travel and lodging expenses. Employers may use video conferencing technology to conduct an interview in which both parties can see, hear, and talk to each other through a video camera and a projection screen. The other method is video interviewing, in which a candidate will be instructed to answer a series of interview questions into a video camera or web cam.

Video conferencing or video interviewing takes a little bit of getting used to at first, so it is a good idea to practice videotaping yourself answering interview questions using a video camera. There are a number of commercial companies that offer Web-based interviewing services to both employers and interviewees, as does *Interview Stream*. Many college career services offices own videotaping equipment or subscribe to a service like *InterviewStream.com*. It would be well worth your while to check with your local college about the availability of mock interviewing services or equipment.

When participating in an interview using distance technology, dress and prepare as if you were going to a live interview. If you will be using conferencing software, you will be able to see your interviewer(s), which will make the process seem more natural once you get used to the technology. If you are expected to answer interview questions into a web cam that does not allow any interaction with the interviewer, then the experience is similar to conducting a telephone interview (except that you do not want to stand up or visually refer to your notes while answering questions). Follow the instructions and look directly into the video camera when answering the questions. Relax, smile, use a conversational tone of voice, and convey a professional image.

Blogs

A blog is an online journal. People use blogs as a diary, as a means of self-expression, as a method to convey information, or as a way to rant about their favorite topic or issue. The information can be helpful or annoying, depending on your perspective.

If you decide to maintain a blog, keep it professional in nature by writing about your research interests, providing professional advice, or writing about environmental concerns, for example.

What Employers Can Find About You

As much as the Internet has helped job seekers find positions, so has it allowed employers to take background checking to new levels. Google yourself to view what information is available—this is what a potential employer will see. In their attempt to hire the best people they can for a position, more and more employers are beginning to conduct Google searches, credit checks, and background checks on potential employees as well as inspect Facebook, MySpace, and LinkedIn profiles. Job seekers, like anyone else who uses the Internet or other communications technology, need to be keenly aware that cyberspace is *not* private and adjust their features and profiles accordingly.

Since an employer can check your employment history, driver's record, and in some states even your criminal record, it is never a good idea to lie on or over-embellish your resume or job application. To protect yourself from unintentional job search self-sabotage, check your own credit rating, modify your social networking profiles, and delete any pictures or information that may potentially harm your employment chances. That goes double for e-mail addresses and voicemail messages that contain language that might make a poor first impression with an employer.

Chapter 15

DECODE JOB DESCRIPTIONS

As long as one keeps searching, the answers come.

Joan Baez

USING THE TRADITIONAL CLASSIFIED SECTION

Although we live in a high-speed digital world, some traditional employment search methods never go out of style. Do not overlook the usefulness of classified ads in your job search. Being able to skillfully navigate through classified ads will give you an advantage over other applicants vying for the same position. The key to using the classifieds is knowing how they are organized and what to look for within the content.

Ads are usually organized by job, industry, or career type. For example, receptionist, executive secretary, or office positions are located under the "Clerical" category. However, if you are looking for an office-related position in the health care industry, such as medical billing, you may also want to look under the "Medical" section.

Business-related positions are usually listed under the "Business" or "Management" sections. If you are looking for a position in hospitality management, you would look under the "Hotel/Restaurant" or "Hospitality" sections as well as at the supervisory jobs. However, sometimes employers in such industries will place their ads seeking managers under the category titled "Management." Therefore, you should check both sections for possible openings.

Your job is to figure out, as best you can, what an employer is going to want in a potential candidate. To gauge what the employer wants, complete the following tasks:

1. Read the title. The title tells you something about the position and the level of responsibility.
2. Read the job description. Take note of the level, duties, responsibilities, skills needed, and personal traits desired. Tailor your resume and cover letter to the requirements listed in the job description.
3. If you are not sure of the common job requirements of a particular position, research the position on the Internet.

Target Your Resume to the Ad

Being able to decode job titles and job descriptions in advertised openings is the key to targeting your cover letter and resume in a way that will entice the employer to invite you in for an interview. You will have more success if you respond to newspaper ads that spell out in detail the qualifications the advertisers are seeking.

Consider the following example of an ad that is too general:

Seeking someone with good people and administrative skills for a busy office. Fax resume to 507.345.4567.

This ad does not provide enough information for you to determine whether you are qualified for, or even want, the position. What do "administrative" skills mean? They could be anything from typing correspondence to preparing reports and budgets. The ad does not specify the type of office setting, the customer population, what the job duties are, or what skills or knowledge are required. Because there is no address listed, you cannot even look up the company to gather any additional information. Since many people may think they have so-called people and administrative skills, they will apply for this job opening, decreasing your chances even further.

Consider the following example of an ad that is more specific:

Busy insurance company seeks a career-minded administrative assistant with proficiency in Microsoft Word, Excel, Power Point, and Access. Must have excellent customer service and organizational skills.

This ad provides all the information you need to (a) determine whether you have the qualifications necessary to successfully compete for the position and (b) target your cover letter and resume to meet the requirements of the position. This ad contains many important details about the position. It tells you the position is an administrative assistant−level position in an insurance office. The skills required are Microsoft Office, customer service, and organizational skills. Note that the employer is looking for someone with "excellent" customer service and organizational skills, not "good" or "I-can-get-by" skills. By noting the word "busy," you can infer that the work environment is a fast-paced (probably high customer traffic) office setting, which could mean that the workload is also heavy. Given this information and the fact that the job is in the insurance industry, one could reasonably assume that the job will entail answering and resolving customer services questions from existing and potential clients and that the employer would want someone who can prioritize projects, possess a friendly, professional customer service demeanor, be able to adapt to changing situations, and multi-task. Furthermore, the addition of the phrase "career-minded" further implies that the employer is looking for someone who will view this job as a long-term commitment and will stay and grow with the company.

Now consider the following example of an ad that is very specific:

Position Title: FT Title III Coordinator: Grant Funded from October 1, 2009, thru September 30, 2014

Position Classification: Full-Time Faculty 12 Month

Academic Rank: Assistant Professor

Minimum Position Qualifications:
1. **Education:** Master's degree in Counseling or a closely related field from a regionally accredited institution.
2. **Experience:** Three (3) years' appropriate work experience in counseling, preferably in a college setting.
3. **Skills:** Strong interpersonal skills, personal, career and transfer counseling, and demonstrated organizational skills.

Position Responsibilities:

Counsels students on educational, occupational, and personal matters. Assists in the organization and implementation of student orientation programs for evening and off-campus sites. Recommends courses for students in advance of and during each registration period. Available for consultation with faculty and administration regarding issues related to the Title III grant. Gathers and maintains educational and occupational information for counseling purposes. Assists in the transfer of students to other institutions of higher education. Assists in evaluation and follow-up studies of various aspects of the College's counseling services. Collaborate with Student Support Services Department to coordinate tutorial programs for evening and off-campus sites. Collaborate with Student Development Department to provide similar services in all such areas as Admissions, Financial Aid, Advising, and Tutoring. Develop and coordinate workshops for evening and off-campus sites. Perform other related duties as assigned by the Associate Dean of Counseling and Student Support Services.

Entry Salary: Assistant Professor, $42,433.00

Standard Work Week: 40 Hours (Position requires evening and some weekend hours. Monday–Friday, 12:00 a.m. to 8:00 p.m.)

Please send a cover letter, resume, three (3) letters of recommendation, and a copy of your official transcripts to (Name and Address of College), Attn: Human Resources Department, on or before 08/21/2010. No phone inquiries, please.

The foregoing is an example of a very detailed advertisement that clearly outlines the education, skills, and experience the employer wants in a candidate. This is the best type of ad because it gives you everything you need to know to target your resume and cover letter and to prepare you for the interview. From this ad, you already know the details of the starting salary and the work hours (12–8 p.m.). Job seekers who are not in a position to work evenings can discard this job opening ad and refocus their efforts on another position. The amount of detail in this ad is also an indication that potential candidates who do not have the listed requirements will be immediately screened out during the initial phase of the search process.

The Assistant Professor position specifically states that the institution is looking for someone who has a master's degree in Counseling. Unless you possess that degree, there is no reason for you to apply. However, the addition of the phrase "or closely related field" does provide some leeway, but what exactly is a "closely related field"? A little research will reveal that the recognized professional standard for college counselors and advisors is a Master's degree in Counseling (a Bachelor's degree in Counseling does not exist). The only other professional degree that could be considered "related" or that would qualify you for a college counseling position would be in Psychology, Student Personnel Services, or Human Services. Any other degree (Education, Business, etc.) would not be acceptable.

From the "experience" and "skills" sections, you know that an applicant would have to have *at least* three years of experience in personal, career, and transfer counseling with students in a college setting. College-setting experience is "preferred," meaning if all other factors are equal, preference would go to the candidate who had prior experience in a college setting. However, *preferred* does not necessarily rule out those applicants who have previously worked in an employment, rehabilitation facility, or other type of community-based social services setting. Applicants working in such settings could strengthen their case by emphasizing any college connections they have had, such as working with local colleges to transition students to a college setting.

Lastly, note that the ad specifically outlines the method for applying—cover letter, resume, three (3) letters of recommendation, and a copy of your official transcripts—by a deadline of 9/21/2010. In other words, failure to follow those instructions will probably disqualify you as an applicant.

The position description contains information that should be pulled out of your relevant past work experience and included in your resume. You have enough information in the ad to form a good idea of what the position will entail. Here is what you can deduce from the ad: This is a grant-funded position (not a permanent position) that will serve college students (traditional-aged and adult students diverse in age, ethnic, and religious backgrounds) from 12 p.m. to 8 p.m. The candidate will therefore be serving both evening and daytime students, all of whom will each have different needs.

As a job seeker, you want to pull out any past work experiences (or college-related experiences if you returned to school for a new degree) that in your capacity as a counselor (personal and/or career counseling) or academic advisor involved providing students with direct services or such group services as orientations and workshops; coordinating large group activities (student orientation, tours, open houses, field trips, etc.); recordkeeping, which implies organization and confidentiality; and any experience with student tutorial needs. The statement "student orientation programs for evening and off campus sites" provides a clue to a possible interview question regarding the differing needs of students who attend during the day, when the population is primarily traditional-aged students but could include some adults, versus those who attend evening classes, whose population is primarily composed of working adults but could include some traditional-aged working students. Any familiarity with writing, administering, or working under a grant should be highlighted, as should any familiarity with other college departments like Admissions, Financial Aid, and Academic Advising. Travel will be an essential requirement of the position, and you can assume that indicating a willingness to travel will get you through the screening process.

Employers are generally concise and specific in ads because words cost money. So, the words that are present in an ad mean something. If the ad indicates, for example, that you must have a specific license, certification, or other earned qualifications, be sure your credentials are in keeping with the requirements and are up-to-date. Make sure you use the current industry keywords and the correct terminology for your field or industry. The best place to research current industry-speak is to look at current job advertisements. You can view current job ads through doing a Google search for a particular job or career or by viewing job descriptions on any of the large job search sites like Indeed.com or Hotjobs.yahoo.com.

Many people list on their resume or in their cover letter the technology, equipment, or procedures they have used, but they fail to indicate how the technology, equipment, or procedures were used or what they were able to accomplish using the technology, for example. Take the next step and illustrate what company problems you helped solve or what goals you accomplished by using specific software, for instance, so the prospective employer can begin to imagine what you can do at his or her company. That's what employers are looking for.

If the ad states a salary, chances are there is no room for negotiation. However, if the ad states a salary range based on experience, this indicates that the compensation package is open for discussion.

If you are in a field that is short on available workers, such as nursing, you should study the ads for "perks." For example, some health care employers offer nurses signing bonuses or other incentives. Read all the ads carefully to maximize your income, benefits, and extras, including flexible work schedules and choices in work environments.

Once you have determined the ads to which you will respond, make sure you carefully read the instructions for applying. If the ad states you must submit your resume to a post office box, do not attempt to e-mail your resume for the sake of expediency. If the ad suggests you must prove you have certain credentials or licenses, make sure you have the documentation. If the ad specifically states, "No phone calls, please," then do not annoy the employer by calling.

Responding in a timely fashion is the key to success in responding to a classified ad. If you see a new opening in the Sunday classifieds, you must act quickly and apply within that week. A nursing recruiter recently told me that her agency removes their ads from CareerBuilder after five days because of the heavy volume of applicants they receive. So it pays to act quickly.

There are some occupations in which no specific major is required. In other words, you can obtain that positions from a variety of majors and backgrounds, but the key is that you must have the work experience. In college settings, admissions personnel must have a Bachelor's or Master's degree, but the area of study really does not matter. The applicant could be a history major, an education major, or a social science major. What does matter is that the individual enjoys working with young people and their parents, is articulate, and is personable.

As a career changer, your task is to "reframe" your past experience to selectively emphasize transferable skills, experience, and knowledge that can immediately apply to the job opening and to deemphasize those skills or experiences that are no longer relevant. Use the information in the job description as a guide to match your skills as closely as possible to the requirements of the job. Be sure you know what an employer is looking for in your new career, and use the current jargon (keywords) in your industry.

Chapter 16

How to Create and Use a Portfolio

Put yourself on view. This brings your talents to light.

Baltasar Gracian

Who Should Use a Portfolio?

A portfolio can be a very powerful tool in an interview. Traditionally, portfolios have been used by artists and writers to showcase their work to potential employers. Today, portfolios are being used by job seekers in all different fields, including education, counseling, engineering, and advertising, as well as by people who create, design, develop, or prepare something as part of their job.

A portfolio is a visual demonstration of your work that illustrates your experiences and activities, training and preparation, and skills and accomplishments. A portfolio is "visual show and tell," used to provide supporting evidence of your skills and abilities during a job interview. A few basic suggestions can help you start thinking about how to put your portfolio together and how to use a portfolio effectively in the job search process.

Items to Include in a Portfolio

Gather together examples and documentation of your accomplishments and skills, assignments, internships, special training, workshops, volunteer work activities, committees, and other activities in your life.

Consider the following possible items to include:

- Resume
- College transcripts
- Licensure or certification documentation
- Memberships to professional organizations
- Positive evaluations
- Letters of recommendation
- Philosophy statement
- Personal mission statement
- Examples of program development
- Grants and proposals

- Photographs or copies of design or other artwork
- Promotional DVDs
- Writing samples
- Class projects
- Evidence of awards or honors
- Laboratory reports
- Synopses of a research paper
- Publications
- Certificates of attendance at seminars or workshops
- Documentation of leadership experience
- Agendas of meetings you conducted
- Flyers or other promotional materials you designed
- Evidence from volunteer, internship, or paid experiences
- Computer disc with examples of work
- Reports on topics of special interest
- Outlines, handouts, or multimedia presentations
- Samples of Web pages

Organizing a Portfolio

Although there are many different ways to organize your portfolio, depending on your experiences and activities and the field in which you are seeking a position, portfolios are generally organized by skills or knowledge areas. Another method is to use the job description of the position for which you are interviewing to help you decide what to include. If the job description asks for teamwork, public speaking, and computer and communication skills, organize your items by those skill areas.

The following categories commonly included in a portfolio:

1. *Professional Statement, Work Philosophy, or Career Goals*
   A statement of your beliefs about yourself and your professional goals as well as your outlook on life in your career area. After reading the statement, an employer should know whether you fit the "style" of the organization. Such a statement is more in-depth than a job objective and can be listed with bullets.
2. *Resume or Vita*
   A copy of your updated, skills-based resume or curriculum vitae.
3. *Transcripts*
   A copy of all college transcripts.
4. *Certificates, Diplomas, Degrees, Honors, Awards, or Special Recognition*
   Copies of your originals or newspaper clippings or pictures.
5. *References*
   A list of professional references or any written letters of recommendation.

6. *Skill Areas or Work Samples*

   Writing samples, artwork, research papers, reports, articles, Web pages, architectural designs, electrical schematics, flowcharts, brochures, flyers, posters, and class projects. For large pieces of artwork or sculpture, take good-quality photographs and include the photo or digital image.

7. *Professional Memberships*

   Copies of membership cards, documents, or letters to show your membership, involvement, and participation.

8. *Awards*

   Any citations, certificates, pictures of medals or trophies, honorable mentions, newspaper articles, photos, or any other type of accolade recognizing you for an accomplishment, no matter how small.

9. *Publications*

   Copies of articles, papers, newsletters, chapters in books, or bylines you have written. If you have written a book, include a copy of the cover page.

10. *Presentations*

    Power Point notes, outlines, conference presentations, workshops, programs, or anything else that shows what you have presented.

11. *Conference Attendance or Continuing Education Participation*

    Nametags, attendance forms, programs, or any type of documentation to show your participation related to attending professional conferences or earning continuing education or professional development credits.

12. *Community Service*

    Photos, newspaper articles, thank you letters, flyers, agendas, certificates of participation, project reports, records of sales, and any other tangible items that highlight community service projects you have been involved with over the years.

13. *Miscellaneous*

    Anything else that you feel is relevant to the position you are applying for or that might elicit interest or conversation during the interview.

Remember, the foregoing categories are a just guide to get you started. Use some or all of the categories as appropriate. Feel free to create additional sections of your portfolio as you see necessary. Your portfolio is unique to you and what you can bring to a company or organization. Do not be afraid to highlight *all* aspects of your skills!

PORTFOLIO DESIGN

When presenting your portfolio to a prospective employer, you should include only the items needed to apply for that particular position. Organize items in a three-ring binder or buy a professional portfolio case that can be purchased from any art or office supply store. Whatever you choose, it should be of good quality and look professional.

Here are additional guidelines to help you get started:

- Use clear plastic sleeves to protect your materials and make them easier to organize and see.
- Prepare a good-size portfolio, which would be approximately 10–20 pages.
- Include a table of contents to help direct readers to particular items and provide a general idea of how the portfolio is organized.
- Use tabs to highlight areas indicated in the table of contents.
- Include captions on every piece of evidence in the portfolio. Captions work best when they are concise, specific, and eye-catching.

You may want to consider creating a computerized version of your portfolio, also known as an "e-portfolio." You could put your portfolio on the Internet to advertise your expertise and availability for a job; bring a stand-alone version on a laptop to the interview, or copy it on a CD that can be left with an employer or selection committee. If you really want to get fancy, you could showcase your skills by adding sound bits, video clips, and animation.

USING A PORTFOLIO DURING THE INTERVIEW

Let your portfolio do the talking in the interview. Use your portfolio to demonstrate abilities, skills, and accomplishments and to support your responses to interview questions. To use the portfolio effectively, think about the type of questions that will likely be asked in your interview. Then, organize your portfolio so that it is a compact visual representation of your professionalism. Practice interviewing while using your portfolio so you will be able to access your portfolio smoothly and quickly in response to an interviewer's questions.

Add and subtract items as the need arises. Reorganize and edit your portfolio to suit each position and company. Your portfolio may change from employer to employer. Research each potential employer's needs and then incorporate any work you have done that relates to what you learn.

Chapter 17

PREPARE FOR
THE INTERVIEW

Failure to prepare is preparing to fail.

Anonymous

The selection process generally begins by advertising an opening, goes on to requesting and reviewing resumes of possible candidates, and then progresses to a process of narrowing down the applicant pool through a series of interviews until the final candidate is selected. In each step of the process, the goal is to weed out applicants who may initially appear qualified for a position but upon further review appear to be unsuited for the position. All of us have heard about potential candidates who looked great on paper but who turned out to be less than what was anticipated in the interview. Remember, as stated earlier in this book, the purpose of the resume is to get an interview. Once a job seeker passes the initial screening, the next goal is to successfully progress through each stage of the interviewing process until you are offered the position. The resume gets you to the interview, but it's in the interview where the real work begins.

Some positions may involve only one or two intermediary steps before the job offer, whereas others (usually the higher-level executive or CEO positions) may involve four or five levels of interview. At the college where I work, it is common to invite a potential college president to participate in a telephone screening, a small meeting with the search committee at the airport, and then a day-long interview on campus in which the interviewee meets with the selection committee, faculty, students, administrators, and the board of trustees. In addition to the normal post-interview reference and credential checks, some colleges will even conduct a follow-up visit to the candidate's current place of work. Now that's an interview! Hopefully, you will not have to endure anything quite so elaborate.

WHEN DOES THE INTERVIEW BEGIN?

If you thought the interview begins when you initially meet the hiring manager on the day of your scheduled appointment, you would be mistaken. The interview begins at the initial point of contact with the company. That includes the initial telephone call to set up the interview appointment, an e-mail inquiry, when you are sitting in the waiting room before for an appointment, or interacting with the secretary or receptionist. With each contact you make with a potential employer, you are providing information about yourself and adding to the opinion he or she is forming about you—even before you meet face-to-face! Therefore, you need to be on your professional game anytime you make contact with the employer. If you make the mistake of being curt or dismissive to the receptionist, that may get back to the hiring manager and sabotage your chances for winning the position.

TYPES OF INTERVIEWS

If you have not interviewed for a job in quite a while, you may not be accustomed to such current interviewing methods as a behavior-based interview questions or objective skills or personality testing.

Traditional Interview

In general, most interviews last one hour or less. However, depending on the level of the position you are applying for, your interview can range from 30 minutes to several hours to several days. A candidate may initially interview with someone from the human resources department, followed up by a direct supervisor, current employees, the boss's boss, the head of the department, or a formal search committee of three to six people. I remember the first interview I went through for a summer position on a pick-your-own strawberry farm. I distinctly remember being asked why I wanted to work there. Luckily for me, I had been coached in advance by a friend who was already working there, so I knew what to say and ended up getting the job (which actually turned out to be one of the better jobs of my youth). In contrast, when I was in college, I applied for a summer job at the local McDonald's, a process that consisted of filling out an application, then immediately being interviewed for 15 minutes by a manager who gave me a decision on the spot and told me I could start the next day. In the Allied Health field, for example, it's not uncommon to spend some time job shadowing one of the staff or having a "working interview" in which you are required to demonstrate some of your abilities by performing a dental hygiene procedure.

The Group Interview

In a group interview situation, make sure you introduce yourself to everyone in the group. If possible, sit across from the lead interviewer. Sometimes the lead interviewer will ask all the questions, or the questions may be split up among the group members. When answering a question, begin and end answering the questions by acknowledging the person who asked you the questions but direct your answer to all the members of the group.

The Behavioral Interview

Behavior-based interviews are those in which the interviewer asks situational questions to evaluate your candidacy for the position. Behavioral interviews have been shown to be more reliable predictors of an interviewee's future on-the-job behavior than are traditional interviewing methods. Consider these examples of typical behavioral interview questions: "What would you do in a particular situation," or "Give me an example of how you would handle an irate customer," or "Suppose you saw a client exhibiting these symptoms, what would you treat first?"

The Telephone Interview

Many employers will use a telephone interview to initially screen potential candidates. Telephone interviews are generally shorter than traditional face-to-face interviews and are designed to narrow the applicant pool to a small, manageable number of individuals who can be invited in for a live interview.

The difficulty with telephone interviews is that you cannot see the people who are talking to you. Therefore, you cannot see their facial expressions or judge how your answers are coming across. For many people, this is a strange experience that takes some getting used to.

The following tips will help you perform your best during a telephone interview:

- Conduct the telephone call in a room that is quiet, has good lighting, and is free of background noise like barking dogs or playing children.
- On a table or counter in front of the phone, lay out a copy of your resume or notes about things to remember to say. If you are asked questions about your background, you'll find it much easier to give quick and accurate responses if you have your resume right in front of you.
- Stand up while you speak on the phone. Doing this will not only help you feel more in control of the situation but allow for good diaphragmatic breathing, which will help you remain calm and give your voice a deeper, fuller sound.
- Smile when you speak and use a pleasant, professional voice. Believe it or not, your facial expressions carry over into your voice.
- Keep your answers clear, concise, and positive. Take a moment to collect your thoughts to think about what you are going to say in response to a question. Avoid the temptation to rush.
- Make sure you answer the question that is asked. Do not waste valuable time by rambling, elaborating, or getting off track and telling stories. Provide examples, but keep your illustrations brief and to the point.

Personality and Basic Skills Testing

Many employers are now relying on such objective measures as personality tests, tests of basic skills, or other instruments to gauge a candidate's personality and characteristics as part of the selection process. Some assessments are aptitude tests, which test basic math, English comprehension, or communication skills. Others are intended to measure honesty or an individual's values. You will be more successful if you approach ethics- or values-based questions by answering very conservatively. For example, the answer to such a question as "Is it all right to steal food if you are starving?" is always no.

Just to get you an example of the extent to which business are using objective measures to screen candidates, consider the following example. One call center near my place of work typically has a four-part job selection process that consists of completing an online application, a telephone screening interview, a face-to-face interview consisting of a personality and aptitude test followed by a 10-minute simulated customer service exercise, and a final face-to face traditional interview. This company hires a large number of employees but has a high turnover rate of employees. Therefore, the company spends a lot of time and resources to select candidates who will ultimately stay at their jobs and perform well for the organization.

BE PREPARED

Everyone is naturally going to be nervous in an interview situation. Even seasoned interviewees will experience a few butterflies the morning before an important interview. The best way to decrease your anxiety level is to be prepared. Let me repeat that again: BE PREPARED FOR THE INTERVIEW. Being prepared for the interview means that you have done your research on the company and the position, you know what kind of interview questions to expect, and you already have an established repertoire of responses (see the following chapter). The more prepared you are for an interview situation, the more confident you will be.

A pharmaceutical sales manager recently told me that if you know the answers to the questions, you will be confident. Enlist the help of a career counselor at your local college or seek a professional career coach. Set up mock interview situations with a trusted friend or family member. Practice delivering your responses in front of the mirror. There are tons of interviewing resources on the Internet. You can even find sample interviewing questions for your particular field. Practice doing mock interviews with a friend or a family member. Videotaping yourself is a highly effective way to improve your interviewing skills. Many people are very uncomfortable watching themselves on videotape, but doing so is the quickest and most effective way to improve your delivery style. Today, there are commercial companies like *InterviewStream.com* that will allow subscribers to record themselves answering interview questions using a web cam; the recording can then be replayed for self-evaluation.

Practice is the key to becoming an effective interviewee. The more interviews you participate in and the more questions you are exposed to, the more comfortable (and successful) you will be during the interview process.

RESEARCH THE COMPANY

One of the most important steps in preparing for an interview is to learn everything you can about the company. Find out as much about the position as you can so you can ask intelligent questions during the interview and position yourself as the candidate best suited for the position.

Most interviewers ask job candidates why they want the job or why they want to work for their company. Most applicants answer this question in terms of why they think their skills are a good match for the position. This does not say anything about why you want to work for the company. Every employer wants an employee who wants to work for *them*, not just for the money or the position. Researching the company before you interview will give you the information you need to formulate an answer tailored to the unique needs or features of the company.

Another reason for researching a company is to be able to make a decision about whether or not to work for that company if offered the position. Knowing all you can about the company will help you decide if you like the direction the company is heading, the job duties, the atmosphere, and the relative health of the company.

WHAT SHOULD YOU BRING TO THE INTERVIEW?

Bring along a copy of your resume (do not assume that your interviewer already has a copy), a list of references that can be handed to the employer when requested, your portfolio if appropriate, a list of questions, and a notepad and pen to take notes. Artists, graphic designers, architects, teachers, and marketing and sales specialists should bring a portfolio that contains representative samples of their creativity, artistic range, and past projects. The use of a portfolio is discussed in Chapter 16.

APPEARANCE

When you dress for an interview, your goal is to look the part of the type of employee the interviewer would want to have representing his or her company. Business casual is commonly worn in most companies today, but that does not mean sloppy. If you need to improve your wardrobe and appearance, do so, but be reasonable. You do not have to go out and get a "nip and tuck" to improve your chances of getting a job. If you are in the television or communications industry, then unfortunately, it may pay to improve your outward image because that industry does favor younger-looking personalities. If you are in any other business and you are feeling unattractive and overlooked by employers despite your experience, you would be better off saving your money and spending your time and energy on bolstering your self-confidence and improving your verbal communication skills. Self-confidence radiates from within.

Business Casual Attire

Consider these tips about how to dress appropriately for your interview:

- Err on the side of conservative.
- Present a tailored look.

- Wear a jacket, or at least bring one along with you.
- Do not wear tight, baggy, or sexually suggestive clothing.
- Make sure tops cover the abdomen.
- Remember, tennis shoes and flip flops are not business casual.

Lack of appropriate attire signals a lack of desire for the position. If you are applying for a position in a creative industry, it is permissible to show a little more of your personality through color or accessories. Some start-up Internet companies value a relaxed atmosphere and encourage creativity. Wearing a conservatively stiff, three-piece suit will not impress them. So it pays to do your research to find out the appropriate culture of the business you are applying to so you will know how to dress.

ASK QUESTIONS

Yes, the interview is your opportunity to have a dialogue to find out what you need to know about the company in order to make an informed decision. Employers expect you to ask intelligent, thoughtful questions. In fact, they will often ask, "Do you have any questions for me?" Sitting there quietly shows that you are not invested in the position. In sales, it is expected that you will try to "close the deal," so go ahead and ask when the interviewer expects to make a decision or ask any other questions you may have.

Do not monopolize the conversation, of course, though most employers expect you to ask questions and will usually allow time for them after the formal interview questions.

During the interview, you will want to gather the following information:

- What are the duties required of the position?
- Who would you be reporting to?
- Why is the position open?
- What are the expectations? Can you describe a typical day?
- Is there room for advancement?
- Does the company provide tuition reimbursement or professional development?
- What is the company or department's philosophy, customer base, annual sales, level of research or laboratory support, or budget allocation? Keep in mind that some of these questions can be answered by researching the company's Web site prior to interview.

The way to ask questions about advancement without appearing ready to jump ship is by qualifying them, perhaps adding, "I want to keep growing professionally. Do you offer any professional advancement opportunities?" or "Once I have proven myself in this position, I would be interested in advancement. What is the company's policy about advancing and promoting its employees?"

There are more subtle ways to determine how people get along in the company or to gauge the stress level in the position instead of asking outright. Sometimes, employers will give you a tour of your office or the company, which will allow you to check out the physical arrangements as well as your coworkers or potential boss. If you do not receive a tour, you can still gain quite a bit of information by watching the interaction between staff as you sit in the reception area. You can gauge the busyness of the office by noting the volume of customers coming through the doors, the number of employees, and the pace at which people seem to operate while performing their jobs. Are people friendly and relaxed, do they seem to enjoy their jobs? Or are they tense, curt, or appear rushed? Ask enough questions to gather the type of information you need to determine if the job for which you are interviewing is a position you want to accept. Gathering this type of information will help take some of the risk out of changing your career.

Chapter 18

INTERVIEW WITH CONFIDENCE

Practice as if you are the worst, perform as if you are the best.

Anonymous

Most people feel uncomfortable "selling" themselves. People, especially women, often feel that marketing themselves will be perceived as "selfish" or even "bragging" or that it's just "not nice to talk about oneself." But suppose you had to sell your house. I bet that you would have no problem clicking off a list of features about your home: charming three-bedroom split level with a large kitchen off a beautiful new sunroom. The same goes for selling yourself to an employer, except that you are selling the features of your work and educational experience. Do not just *tell* the interviewer that you are a self-starter or creative. Show him or her what you did to demonstrate these characteristics and let the data speak for you.[1]

Review your 30-second commercial (see Chapter 4). It is not bragging to describe your work experience in terms of having "over 16 years of quality, results-oriented customer service in a financial services environment" or by describing yourself as a "well organized individual, attentive to detail, with the ability to resolve customer conflicts." Of all the social situations we encounter in our lives, rest assured that the interview *is* the appropriate place to brag. By carefully selecting your words, you can sell yourself by describing your positive qualities in a way that will not turn other people off. Another way to look at it is to describe yourself as a friend would describe you. In an interview situation, it is your job to educate the interviewer about your skills and abilities. Do not sell yourself short by assuming the interviewer will be able to discern your true worth. So, in front of a mirror or to a friend or spouse, begin practicing answering the following questions until you feel comfortable saying them out loud:

1. My strengths are: _____, and _____.
2. I have ____ years of _____ experience in _____ and _____.
3. My educational background is _____.
4. One of my greatest accomplishments is when I _____.
5. The one area I would like to improve in is _____.
6. I would be a good candidate for your position because _____.
7. You should hire me because I _____.

RELATE YOUR PAST TO YOUR FUTURE

Use all your transferrable skills, as well as your current knowledge or training, to best match your background to the position in your new career. Read the job description, then pick out examples of your past work or educational experience that directly apply to the skills listed in the job description. If you are applying for a customer service position that entails interviewing applicants, for example, give examples of any previous job where you surveyed, interviewed, or elicited responses from customers or clients. It helps to think like an employer: what traits or experience would you want an employee to have for this position? If your career change resulted in going back to school for training but you do not have any practical work experience, use your internship, volunteer work, or clinical, practicum, field work, class project, service learning, or any other educational-related experiences to cite examples. Use the experiences you do have, paid or unpaid.

SHOW ENTHUSIASM

Show some enthusiasm for the position. Employers are often concerned that older job applicants lack the energy and motivation for work. The best way to show that you have not lost your drive is to display some passion during the interview. Body language is equally important as, if not more important than, your words. Lean slightly forward in your chair when the interviewer is speaking. Maintain appropriate eye contact. Appear alert. Respond with an intelligent question. Use your age to imply knowledge and experience while conveying energy and enthusiasm.

PRACTICE

When it comes to interviewing, practice makes all the difference. Anticipate the kinds of commonly asked interview questions for your field and practice how to respond to those questions well before the interview. Granted, you may not be able to anticipate every question an interviewer will throw at you, but you can preformulate your answers to the most commonly asked questions. Practice drawing examples from your extensive background to answer commonly asked questions about how you approach and solve a problem, how you work with others, your management style, your accomplishments, and your strengths and weaknesses. How employers perceive you is partially determined by how you present and sell yourself.

Commonly Asked Interview Questions

Practice answering the following frequently used questions:

1. "Tell me about yourself."
2. "How have your educational and work experiences prepared you for this position?"

3. "What are your strengths?" "What are your weaknesses?"
4. "Why are you interested in working here?"
5. "Describe a situation where you had a conflict with another individual, and tell how you dealt with it."
6. "Describe your leadership style."
7. "Tell me about a difficult decision you have made."
8. "What do you think you can contribute to this company?"
9. "What characteristics are most important in a good manager?" "How have you displayed one of these characteristics?"
10. "Describe an accomplishment that has given you the most satisfaction."

Candidates for management or administrative positions may be asked, "What would you do during the first week on your job?" or "What types of problems would you expect to encounter during your first month of work?" Such questions are a perfect example of questions that will require some prior research of the company or at least a familiarity with the types of problems and issues common to that industry. Doing your research will allow you to prepare a reasonable speculative response.

Career practitioners recommend that job seekers "practice" their interviewing skills during such "less crucial" interviewing situation as career or job fairs. Once you have gone through a few industry-specific interviews, you'll develop a repertoire of common questions that most interviewers ask.

JOB INTERVIEW JITTERS

A little nervousness is normal before and during an interview. Employers understand this, and even they might be a little nervous. A little bit of adrenaline is valuable because it can give you the edge you need and may actually enhance your ability by giving you the appearance of having enthusiasm and energy. Too much anxiety shuts down the thought processes and clouds the mind. Breathe deeply, relax, and just do your best. Think positively, and slow your speech down a little if you have a tendency to talk too fast when nervous.

For some people, it helps to think of the person interviewing you as an equal, not a superior. Think of the interview as one of *many* opportunities. People put too much pressure on themselves by telling themselves that they absolutely "have" to win this job. The paradox is that if they would scale back the level of importance placed on the job, they would feel more relaxed and probably perform better in the interview. Sometimes jobs are won or lost because of factors that have nothing to do with you, so just do your best, learn from the experience, and move on.

RECOVERING FROM A "BAD" INTERVIEW

If you flub or blow a question during the interview, it is very common to become flustered, which ends up ruining the rest of the interview. We all have "bad" interviews and, unfortunately, that's just part of the process of looking for a job. The most important thing to remember is not to let one "bad" question ruin the rest of the interview. If it happens, try to put it behind you and focus your attention on the next question.

Julie e-mailed me in a panic after having a "bad" interview. She said she was asked a technical question she did not understand, could not answer the question, became flustered, and from then on was not able to communicate that she was the best person for the position.

If you do not know the answer to a question, think "thoughtfully" for a moment and then just answer, "I'm sorry, but I'm not familiar with that." You may want to follow it up with, "Is that critical to this position?" or something to that effect. Usually, the interviewer will provide a short explanation, which gives you enough time to gather your composure and respond. If you do not understand the question, always ask for clarification: "I'm not sure I follow you." Again, asking such questions buys you time. After hearing the explanation, it may be that you do know what the interviewer is referring to and find that you can provide an appropriate response. If you are asked a question you really do not know the answer to, it is always better to be up front and say something like "I'm sorry, but I'm not familiar with that process" in a calm and self-assured way rather than try to fabricate something and look like a fool. Then, go home and look up the answer to that question or rehearse a response so you are prepared for the next time. And there will be a "next time."

Industry- or Profession-Specific Questions

Be prepared to answer in-depth, situational questions specifically related to your profession. For example, a Nursing interviewer may ask any of the following questions:

- What are your strengths and weaknesses in the clinical area?
- What kinds of patients have you provided care for in the medical-surgical area of your education?
- Describe how you would collaborate with other members of the health care team?
- What would you do if you had a question regarding a physician's order?
- What is your experience with patient teaching?
- What would you do if a family member were upset about the nursing care provided for their relative?

Examples of industry-specific interview questions can be found on the Internet.

CHALLENGING QUESTIONS

Be prepared to handle some challenging questions. Remember, it is the interviewer's job to put you on the spot; to make you feel stressed and uncomfortable. Interviewers are just trying to figure out if you are going to be a good employee.

Sometimes interviewers will ask questions designed to see if you will complain or reveal something negative. In response to "What was the worst thing about your last job?" or "Why did you leave your last job?" you want to answer the questions but turn a negative into a positive. For example, "Well, let me see, there really wasn't a 'worst' part of my job, it was just I had been there for so long that I began to feel bored and unchallenged." This type of answer implies that you still have initiative, drive, and the desire to take on new projects. If you are asked why you left a previous position, make your answer a brief, factual statement without emotion, and never whine or bad mouth a previous employer.

Recognize that some questions that are designed to automatically qualify or disqualify you. "Are you willing to relocate?" is a disqualifier. The answer is always either "Yes" or "Under the right circumstances." Do not automatically disqualify yourself unless you are absolutely certain you do not want to accept the position.

There is always the possibility that you'll be asked an unusual question that will throw you for a loop. I remember one interview in which I was asked, "What kind of animal would you want to be?" The wrong answer would have been, "What a stupid question." Instead, I bought myself some time by saying, "That's an interesting question." I think I ended up replying that I wanted to be a wild horse running free in the desert or something along that line. This question is designed to gain some insights into your personality, so you want to pick an animal appropriate to the characteristics you think the employer is looking for in an employee. However, now that I think about it, a better answer might have been, "I do not think I'd want to be anything other than a human animal because of all the things I would be missing out on like . . ." or something similar.

In one form or another, you will be asked about why you decided to make a career change. Formulate your response something like this: "I've always had an interest in . . ." or "When the company began downsizing, I had an opportunity to use my severance pay to go back to school and pursue a new career in . . ." or "I enjoy my current job but am interested in changing career paths. I'd like to expand my knowledge by moving into [blank] department and learning how to . . ." Whatever your response, you will have to convince the employer that you are committed to and excited about your new career change. However you decide to respond, do not badmouth your former position, employer, or industry. As justified as your reasons may be, your responses will only serve to put you in a negative light because an employer will think you are a complainer or someone who has a problem with authority or cannot get along with others.

If you are an older career changer and during the interview hear, "We have a very busy office here" or "Our employees are expected to be flexible," you must address the unspoken concerns regarding your age. Assure the employer that one of the reasons you decided to make a career change at this point in your life was because you were bored or feeling unchallenged. You could also throw in that you are used to fast-paced environments or have been a part of organizations that have had to adapt quickly to market change or administrative restructuring.

If your interviewer seems concerned about your ability to adapt to a new company or being set in your ways, you might say, "I find that I'm motivated by new challenges, and that's one of the reasons I'm so interested in this position," or "Even though I spent the last 12 years in the same company, I held a variety of positions and always welcomed the opportunity to work with new people and learn new skills."

If your interviewer seems concerned that you might be overqualified for a position, stress that you see this position as an opportunity to begin working in your new career field. Deemphasize your many years of experience in your previous profession, but do continue to emphasize your unique attitudes, abilities, and interests that relate to this particular position.

To disarm the "You'll be too expensive" concern, explain that at this point in your life, it is more important to be engaged in the work that you love rather than concerned about the amount of money you'll make (unless of course, you are trying to transition to the sales, finance, or marketing field, in which making money is a priority). If an employer knows that you are making a career change from a high-paying industry, you will need to be prepared to explain that your former salary was appropriate for that career but that you expect to receive a salary that is appropriate for your new career.

SOME FINAL INTERVIEW TIPS

When it comes to the interview, make it all about the company, not about you. If you are asked questions about your personal life, talk about the community projects you are involved with or the last great golf game or tennis match you played. Keep the photos of your pets or the grandkids in your wallet.

Communication skills and presentation style are critical. What you say implies how you think. Convey professionalism, intelligence, confidence, and congeniality. Watch your language and use good grammar, do not use slang or be overly friendly or casual. If you are older, avoid phrases that may date you.

Do not talk about money or benefits before the employer does, or you will give the unappealing impression that salary is all you care about. Let the employer mention salary first. Broaching the subject first implies that you are more interested in money and perks that about doing a good job. Try to think like an employer—all employers want someone who wants to work for them and who will do a good job and represent the company well.

Finally, check your attitude. Be confident but not cocky or arrogant. Even though you may be older (and wiser) than the person interviewing you, do not show an "I've been there and have seen it all before" attitude, even if it's true. There is always something that even you can learn. Spin that attitude into "I have some knowledge that can help you." Remember, you are trying to get a job. While you may want to be impressive, take care not to become overbearing. You will be leave a more lasting impression if you can convey your expertise by speaking in a confident, pleasant, but professional conversational tone of voice and using the type of intelligent, respectful language that does not irritate or offend anyone.

Pre-Interview Checklist

Get yourself off to a good start by using a pre-interview checklist like this one:

___ 1. I have the name, address, and telephone number of the company.
___ 2. I have the name of the person I will interview with.
___ 3. I know how to get to the company.
___ 4. I know what the company does.
___ 5. I have my resume, references, and portfolio.
___ 6. I have my list of questions.
___ 7. I am dressed properly and professionally.

Post-Interview Checklist

After the interview, determine how well you handled yourself. Use a checklist with such questions as these:

___ 1. I arrived for the interview at least 10 minutes early.
___ 2. I greeted receptionist in a friendly manner.
___ 3. I stood and shook hands with a *firm* handshake.
___ 4. I was appropriately and professionally dressed.
___ 5. I did not slouch in the chair.
___ 6. I did not smoke or chew gum.
___ 7. I remembered to leave my cell phone in the car.
___ 8. I gave the interviewer a copy of my resume and references.
___ 9. I maintained good eye contact and attentive body language.
___ 10. I was well prepared.
___ 11. I showed an interest in the company and in the job.
___ 12. I let the interviewer take the lead.
___ 13. I gave clear and concise answers to questions.
___ 14. I avoided slang expressions and poor grammar.
___ 15. I answered questions confidently.
___ 16. I highlighted my strong points and gave examples.
___ 17. I avoided criticism of former bosses or companies.
___ 18. I was a good listener.
___ 19. I maintained good eye contact.
___ 20. I asked pertinent, intelligent questions concerning the job.
___ 21. I volunteered any important information that was overlooked.
___ 22. I understood when and how to follow up after the interview.
___ 23. I thanked the interviewer for his (or her) time and consideration.
___ 24. I let the interviewer know I was interested in the job.
___ 25. I sent a thank you note after the interview.

Post-Interview Self-Assessment Questions

After the interview, also reflect on your interview performance. Doing this will help you determine what you did well and also point out what you could do better for the next interview.

Consider the following self-assessment questions:

1. What questions were difficult for me to answer?
2. What made me uncomfortable during the interview?
3. Which of my responses impressed them the most?
4. What do I wish I had said or done differently?
5. Did I feel like I made a connection with the interviewer?
6. On a scale of 1 to 5 (5 being the best), how do I think the interview went overall?

After a good night's sleep, review your answers and make notes about anything you would do to improve. Hopefully, you'll get a call within the next few days that the job is yours!

Chapter 19

WHAT EMPLOYERS
REALLY WANT

To be trusted is a greater compliment than to be loved.

George MacDonald

WHAT EMPLOYERS LOOK FOR WHEN HIRING NEW EMPLOYEES

To give yourself a competitive edge in the marketplace against candidates of varying backgrounds and experience levels, it helps to know what employers are looking for.

When employers are interviewing candidates, they are essentially looking for three things: (1) does the employee have the skills and knowledge to do the job, (2) is he or she willing to do the job, and (3) will the person fit in with the rest of the staff?

Beyond those questions, there are some universal skills that employers seek in candidates across all job levels that make the difference between being successful and not being successful in the workplace. These skills are often referred to as "soft skills."

According to the National Association of Colleges and Employers (NACE), employers are impressed by job candidates who have great communication skills. They're also looking for motivation and initiative, teamwork skills, leadership abilities, interpersonal skills, analytical skills, and ethics.[1] The following list identifies the top 10 qualities employers look for when hiring:

1. Communication skills (speaking and writing)
2. Honesty and integrity
3. Teamwork skills
4. Interpersonal abilities
5. Strong work ethic
6. Motivation and initiative
7. Flexibility and adaptability
8. Analytical and research skills
9. Computer literacy
10. Organizational skills

Communication Skills. By far, the number one skill mentioned most often by employers is the ability to listen, write, and speak effectively. Successful communication is critical in business. It's the means by which problems are resolved, customers are more satisfied with a product or service, disputes are mitigated, and harmony and teamwork solidified.

Honesty and Integrity. Employers probably respect personal integrity more than any other value, especially after the recent corporate scandals. In light of the public outcry over the Enron and Bernie Madoff scandals, employers are seeking to reestablish the public trust by hiring people who will not end up being a distraction or an embarrassment to their business. Many employers will check a candidate's credit rating as part of the reference-checking process. You do not want to be disqualified for a position because of bad or erroneous information on your credit rating. Check your credit rating using sites like AnnualCreditReport.com, which allows you to fix any erroneous information immediately through the reporting service.

Teamwork Skills. Many projects are run by small groups or committees. You must have the ability to work with others. Even if you do not like or agree with your colleagues, you must be able to set personal differences aside to work together in a professional manner to achieve a common goal.

Interpersonal Abilities. The ability to relate to your coworkers, work well in a team environment, and resolve conflict with coworkers is essential given the amount of time spent at work each day. Employers want employees who will get along with the rest of the team, fit in with office staff, adopt the company culture, and buy into the company philosophy. But mostly employers are looking for someone who has a willingness to work and achieve the goals of the company. Everyone has had the experience of working with coworkers who do nothing but complain or spent too much time talking or gossiping about others. Such situations cause conflict and are disruptive to others.

Strong Work Ethic. Employers seek job seekers who love what they do and will carry their share of the workload, or even go beyond, to finish a task. A strong work ethic includes dependability, reliability, and responsibility. There's no question that all employers desire employees who will arrive to work every day—on time and ready to work—and who will take responsibility for completing their job duties. We all hate the delegator, or the person who gives only half effort during crunch time, or the one who leaves work for others to pick up.

Motivation and Initiative. While teamwork is always mentioned as an important skill, so is the ability to work independently, with minimal supervision. Employers want to know that their employees are doing what they are supposed to do and are following through on their assignments and responsibilities. In the health care industry, for example, an employer must be able to trust that its doctors, nurses, and other health care staff are working with patients in a safe and ethical manner. When employers are confident that their employees are doing their jobs, then they are themselves free to focus on the tasks they need to accomplish that contribute to greater production of the company.

Flexibility and Adaptability. Flexibility and adaptability are simply the ability to manage multiple assignments and tasks, set priorities, and adapt to changing conditions and work assignments. Adaptability is a trait that is quickly becoming an essential competency for survival and success in the American workplace. Employers want people who can (1) problem-solve and generate new ideas or new approaches, (2) be willing to learn new approaches and use changing technology, (3) demonstrate interpersonal adaptability by being able to work effectively in a team made up of diverse members, and (4) cope with work stress by remaining calm in difficult circumstances and being able to cope with uncertainty and ambiguity.

Analytical and Research Skills. Important to employers is their employees' ability to assess a situation, seek multiple perspectives, gather more information if necessary, and identify key issues that need to be addressed.

Computer Literacy. Almost all jobs now require a basic understanding of computer hardware and software, especially word processing, spreadsheets, and e-mail. Being computer literate is now an absolute requirement in almost any job. Everyone must know how to search for information on the Internet, schedule appointments using an electronic calendar system, and communicate by e-mail. Armed with a wireless laptop and a cell phone, many business executives and sales reps only need to find a wireless hot spot to be able to conduct their business. We are living in a time where technology changes at light speed. Unfortunately, employees who cannot adapt to the new technology will simply get left behind in today's workforce.

Organizational Skills. Organizational skills encompass numerous areas, among them the ability to manage tasks and job duties with multiple priorities in a fast-paced busy environment. The ability to keep track of projects, assignments, and customers is a crucial element of a position. As well, the ability to follow up on important phone calls, respond to e-mails in a timely fashion, and meet deadlines is critical to a company's sales, service, or productivity.

Other personal traits that employers seek and that are important to an employee's success in the workplace include:

1. Multicultural awareness and sensitivity
2. Problem-solving/reasoning/creativity
3. Drive and passion
4. Professionalism
5. Willingness to learn

Multicultural Awareness and Sensitivity. There is possibly no bigger issue in the workplace today than diversity, and job seekers must demonstrate a sensitivity and awareness to other people and cultures. Today, the workplace is made up of people from all ages and backgrounds. Between 2000 and 2016, according to the Bureau of Labor Statistics, international migration will account for more than half of our nation's population growth, with the fastest growth in the number of Hispanic and Asian immigrants.[2]

Marketplace globalization, outsourcing, and relaxed trade restrictions have resulted in American companies being owned by, or doing business with, countries in every corner of the world. It is not uncommon for people to conduct business with clients from other countries or for office personnel and administrators to talk with staff at a sister plant in London or Germany. Being able to get along and communicate effectively with workers from different backgrounds and all walks of life has become crucial in today's business world.

Problem-Solving/Reasoning/Creativity. The ability to find solutions to problems using your creativity, reasoning, and past experiences along with the available information and resources is yet another important employee characteristic important to employers.

Drive and Passion. The job seekers who get hired and the employees who get promoted are the ones with drive and passion—and who demonstrate this enthusiasm through their words and actions. Employers want to hire someone who is excited about working for them, not someone who has to find a job.

Professionalism. Professionalism is acting in a responsible and fair manner in all your personal and work activities and following the codes of conduct established by your profession. Being professional means, for example, not crossing personal boundaries with clients or customers, as well as not relating to clients or customers in a rude, overly casual, or disrespectful manner. Professionalism is seen as a sign of maturity and self-confidence. Employers are looking for individuals who can present themselves and the company in a professional manner. Proper telephone etiquette, good customer service manners, and appropriate appearance are highly valued.

Dressing in attire appropriate for that industry's culture is also a part of professionalism. The CEO of a company who is expected to go out into the public to meet with donors and other business professionals needs to dress in a far different manner than someone who is developing software in a casual office setting or running a forklift on a warehouse dock.

I include good customer service as being a part of professionalism. Customer service and proper telephone etiquette in today's world are quickly becoming a lost art. How many of us have had horrible experiences being put on hold or transferred around to several departments when trying to straighten out a billing error. Providing accurate information, not being rude, explaining things in understandable language, and be willing to go the extra mile to help a customer find what he or she is looking for is good customer service. And good customer service makes a difference in a company's bottom line—and ultimately in your paycheck.

Willingness to Learn. No matter what your age or how much experience you have, you should always be willing to learn a new skill or technique. Jobs are constantly changing and evolving, and you must show an openness to grow and learn with that change. Employers do not want to hire someone who has been out of touch with the work world and today's job requirements. You may know yesterday's job requirements perfectly, but yesterday is history. Every field is going through rapid change. Employers need someone who is current in their field because not being able to keep up with change will result in being left behind.

INDUSTRY-SPECIFIC SKILLS

Every employer is looking for a specific set of skills from job seekers that match the skills necessary to perform a particular job. Accountants need to know how to use proper accounting procedures, and educators need to know how to effectively convey information to students. Desired employee traits can be industry-specific. Assertiveness and originality, for example, are more valuable employee traits in sales positions than they are in counseling positions, where listening skills and sensitivity are valued. In a recent NACE survey, government and nonprofit employers preferred potential employees to have creativity and be detail-oriented more so than did manufacturers and service employers, who ranked entrepreneurial skills and sense of humor near the bottom.[3]

Management positions will be looking for someone who has the ability to lead and motivate others to achieve specific goals. They also require someone who is able to plan, prioritize, coordinate projects, and see tasks through to completion. Each profession looks for specific knowledge-based traits in its respective discipline. If you recently changed careers and do not have a lot of real-world work experience in your new field, try to obtain hands-on experience through college courses, clinicals, practica, internships, or volunteer work to gain critical skills.

Possessing the skills that employers are looking for in ideal employees will help you successfully compete for a job opening, even against candidates who have more work experience than you. If you are looking for a position in health care, for example, you can strengthen your candidacy if you can demonstrate that you are ethical, professional, have good people skills, can follow directions, have solid critical thinking skills, and are a team player. Likewise, Graphic Design job seekers can increase the chances of being hired by demonstrating in person, or through a portfolio, that they are highly creative in a variety of mediums, can conceptualize, have good communication skills, and have proficiency in the latest software programs such as the Adobe Acrobat applications.

In the minds of employers, it's all about what *you* can do for *them*. After all, that's why they are hiring you. They are looking for a worthy candidate to replace someone who's left or retired, fill a need in their company, solve a problem, or sell their product. Presenting your education, skills, and prior work experience in a way that illustrates how you used your expertise or knowledge to improve the bottom line, reach more customers, or service more clients will get you noticed. If you are in a service-related industry, employers are looking for people who can establish relationships with potential customers, keep current customers, and provide a quality service or deliver a product. If you are in a skilled industry, employers are looking for people who can troubleshoot, solve a problem, and improve a process that ultimately improves productivity and profit.

Career changers can use their transferrable skills from past work experiences to demonstrate soft skills to a potential employer. A previous position in a customer service industry, for example, can demonstrate ability to establish a good working relationship with people of diverse backgrounds or highlight an ability to resolve disputes. Previous administrative or office positions can provide examples of good organizational skills, customer service, the ability to maintain confidentiality, the ability to meet deadlines, or the ability to multi-task in a fast-paced environment.

Chapter 20

THE SUBJECT OF SALARY

The amount you earn at any time is a reflection of the value that others place upon your contribution.

Brian Tracy

RESPONDING TO REQUESTS FOR SALARY HISTORY

If possible, try to postpone responding to a request for a salary history until a job offer is made. If you must respond, you may want to say something like "Seeking a salary range of $30,000 to $40,000 based on industry standards." If directly asked during an interview, provide a salary range that you found during your job market investigation. You can obtain salary ranges by talking to people who work in the same field, reviewing industry journals and Internet sites, and analyzing comparable jobs. Based on your research, you can provide a salary range in line with the current market.

You may also try asking the interviewer, "What salary range are you working with?" or "I realize you need to be sure my expectations are consistent with the salary range for this position. To make sure we're on the same page, what is the range we're dealing with?" Many times, the employer will have a fixed amount in mind and will answer you. You can then respond, "That is certainly within my salary requirement range," which does not obligate you to that salary but also does not eliminate you from the candidate pool before a final offer is made.

Likewise, when responding to the salary question on an application, you can write, "Open to negotiation," "Flexible," or "Willing to discuss." Again, you want to respond to the question asked but do not want to disqualify yourself by listing a figure that's too high or too low for the position.

FACTORS TO CONSIDER

If you will be relocating, you cannot compare salaries from different geographic areas because the cost-of-living differs from one part of the country to another. Living in New York City, for example, is going to be considerably more expensive than living in Oklahoma or Georgia. See http://www.salary.com for their salary wizard or http://www.bestplaces.net for a cost-of-living comparison between cities across the country.

Management positions generally pay more because they involve more responsibility and incur more consequences if an incorrect decision is made. Sales quotas, the number of hours expected to work, the amount of travel involved, and the numbers of employees supervised are also factors to consider. Some employers will compensate you for what they are asking you to do; others feel no such responsibility to compensate you for what your skill is worth. So you should be aware of your worth. Some companies will promise to increase your pay after a probationary period or when you finish that advanced degree. Get these promises in writing, since promises are often forgotten or management may change.

Market demand is an important factor in determining salary. Employee shortages in a particular field mean that employers will be willing to offer higher salaries to attract workers. This situation can be used to your advantage. Know what the going market value is for your profession and degree. An entry-level salary in nursing, for example, may be higher than some mid-level management positions, so do your research beforehand and know what salary to expect for your geographic area.

CHANGE IN SALARY AFTER A CAREER CHANGE

If you are forced to make a career change because of a layoff, downsizing, or your company moved overseas, and you try to find another job in your current profession or make a career change, your salary may significantly drop simply because you will now be starting at the bottom end of the salary scale of your new career. If you are in your fifties, you may have been at the upper end of your salary and benefits scale when you were laid off, with seniority and lots of accrued vacation and sick days. Unfortunately, you will have to begin at the starting salary for your new profession because employers do not pay for seniority gained at another company. However, because of your wealth of experience, you may be able to start at the upper end of the entry-level salary range and should be able to advance more quickly than a younger, more inexperienced counterpart.

Many older career changers discover that they have to begin their new career at a lower salary than they previously enjoyed. Remember our retail store manager turned college professor career changer? She experienced a 43 percent decrease in salary when she left her field and became an instructor. It took her 10 years to get back to the same level of salary. In a study of career change in 30-year-olds, 70 percent of participants reported a significant drop in salary, but the drop was not seen as a barrier to changing careers.[1] The participants saw their reduced earnings as a temporary situation and a short-term sacrifice in return for doing what they wanted.

If you are anticipating a drastic cut in pay, your choices are to adjust your standard of living or relocate to a geographic area that has a lower cost-of-living. Many people who have changed careers have found they still earn enough money to live on comfortably, after scaling back their expenses, and the perks they gained were worth the decrease in salary.

In the past, people were able to increase their salary by changing jobs or receiving promotions. Given today's economic climate, it is more difficult to do that once you have established a salary at the upper end of your pay scale—but it is not impossible. I personally made a significant increase in salary when I switched educational institutions back in 2000, and I know two college-level CEOs who significantly increased their salaries when they moved to other institutions.

A more common method to substantially increase your salary through a career change is to obtain additional education such as going back to school to become a nurse or continuing on to graduate school. Doing that, of course, assumes the position you left paid less than the position you plan to change your career to.

STARTING SALARY IN YOUR NEW CAREER

Starting salary is critical because all future advances, raises, and promotions are based on that initial amount. You do not want to bring up the subject first; doing so will create an unpleasant impression. If forced to state a figure, give a range based on your living expenses and comparable market value. Be informed about the starting salary and the value of your degree or skills in your particular geographic area. Generally speaking, there is less room for bargaining in entry-level positions than in higher-level positions, where experience can be used to negotiate terms.

Most employers deal with a salary range. They would like to pay you less, but they may be willing to pay more for a candidate they really want. The bottom line is that if you do not ask, you will never know if you can get a higher salary. If salary cannot be negotiated, try negotiating for such other benefits as a flexible schedule or a reduction in health insurance copayments.

In general, wait until you have been offered the position before you attempt to discuss salary. This is the only time you will have any bargaining power. If the interviewer brings up salary, take that as a sign that the company is definitely interested in you. Always begin the negotiation conversation by stating that you are open or flexible on this subject, but negotiate within a particular salary range based on your previous research. Factors to take into considerations are the level of the position, the industry, and the requirements of the position. If you are applying for a sales-related position, where negotiation skills are critical to success, then by all means demonstrate your negotiating skills. However, if you are applying for an administrative position in a company with a rigid salary structure, then there's not much point in negotiating other than to ask if there is any room to move salary.

The advancement potential of a career changer is better than that of a new graduate, even if you go back to school to learn a new profession. Chris, an IT programmer at a large utility company, was one of the many managers who were laid off when his company was sold to another utilities firm. Eventually, Chris was able to find a position at a medical billing company, but as an entry-level programmer. Although the position was well beneath his abilities, he eventually settled in at the company and performed well. After 18 months, per company policy, he was approached by a supervisor in another division who suggested he bid on an opening for a supervisor position. Because of his wealth of experience from his years of work at his former utilities company and his record of good performance at his present job, Chris was able to land the new position and increase his salary. Chris is now on his way to regaining the salary he once enjoyed because he was able to be promoted to a higher level more quickly than a new IT professional or recent grad would have been.

Salary Information

You can consult numerous sources to obtain useful salary information, including employment trends, salary ranges, and demographics to help you. Some useful sources are the following Internet sites:

- **America's Career InfoNet** (http://www.acinet.org). Identifies wage and employment trends for states and occupations as well as demographic and economic information.
- **Bureau of Labor Statistics** (http://www.bls.gov). Provides a wealth of employment information. Select "Wages, Earnings, & Benefits" for salary information for various occupations in your area and elsewhere.
- **City Town Info** (http://www.citytowninfo.com/employment). Is an excellent source of unique facts about cities across the United States, including job salaries.
- **Jobstar** (http://www.jobstar.org). Has links and descriptions to over 300 salary surveys.
- **Salary.com** (http://www.salary.com). Contains "Personal Tools & Resources" with a searchable database for average salaries by occupation and state or metropolitan area.

Chapter 21

AFTER THE INTERVIEW

Success comes from taking the initiative and following up . . . persisting.
Anthony Robbins

After the interview, and before you forget, make some notes about the interview, what questions you were asked, and your impressions of the people and the company in general. If you are offered the position, you will want to review this information when determining whether to accept or not accept the position.

1. Have you been offered a fair salary that is commensurate with your skills, education, and experience? Is it comparable to other positions in the job market? Are there benefits? What is the potential for advancement? Are there any other perks or benefits besides the traditional health and life insurance? What is the commuting distance to and from work? Will you be expected to pay for parking or is parking provided? Will you be reimbursed for travel expenses?

2. Did you meet your potential boss? Did he or she seem like someone with whom you could develop a good working relationship?

3. Did you meet or gather any information about your potential coworkers? Do you know the number of people employed in your department? If you were given a tour of the office during your interview, you probably had a chance to meet your potential coworkers. Do they seem friendly? Will there be any antagonism toward you as a newcomer? Do you think you will be able to get along with, or at least work with, the other people in your office or department?

4. Will you be comfortable in your new setting? Is your office space adequate for your needs? (Do you have an office?) Will a computer be provided? Do you have access to the kind of equipment, supplies, materials, or resources you will need to perform your job? How large is your budget? How many staff will you be expected to supervise? Although some of these factors can often be negotiated at the beginning of your employment, they can sometimes make all the difference between comparable job offers.

5. Is the corporate culture in line with your values and career goals? Are the organization's goals, philosophy, and employee expectations something that you can live with? How many hours per week will you be expected to work? Is overtime optional or mandatory? Is there a dress code?

FOLLOW-UP LETTERS

When you get home from the interview, follow up with a short handwritten (or typed if your handwriting is poor) note or e-mail thanking the interviewer(s) for the opportunity to discuss the position. Reiterate your interest in the position, and use the opportunity to highlight your qualifications or add any additional points you may have forgotten to mention in the interview. If you are not sure who to address the letter to, call the Human Resources Office or the person who originally scheduled the interview and ask for that person's name and title (and the *correct* spelling of his or her name). Thank you letters are another opportunity to create a favorable impression that is often overlooked in today's busy world.

If you receive a phone call from the company offering you the position and you want to accept it, by all means say so and express your enthusiasm for being selected for the position. Ask for details regarding the first day of work, if a pre-employment physical or drug-screening test is required, and when to fill out paperwork for things like life insurance and health benefits. Then, follow the offer up with an acceptance letter or e-mail.

If you are declining an offer, the proper professional response is to say so in writing. Express your appreciation for being selected, and wish the company the best in its search.

JUGGLING MORE THAN ONE OFFER

You may find yourself in the lucky position of receiving more than one job offer. If this happens, you will need to manage the situation without jeopardizing either offer. Explore the possibility of delaying the offers with each employer to give you time to consider their offers. Do not stretch out the waiting game any longer than necessary. Keep in mind that you do not have the same level of bargaining power in your new career that you did in your past one because you do not have the same level of experience. Sometimes, it's best to just be honest and say, "I am really interested in your position, but I have received an offer from another company that I am equally interested in and the hiring manager is offering me X dollars more in salary. Are you able to match that?" If they are, they will say so and that may settle the issue. If they are not, you will know that up front and can accept the other position accordingly. In either scenario, most employers will appreciate your honesty.

Each profession will have specific job-related factors that are important considerations when choosing to accept a position. In the nursing profession, for example, factors to consider are the type of shift available (usually beginning or "graduate" nurses begin on second shift), number of staff on a floor, availability of overtime, type of patients, the nurse-to-patient ratio, quality of the facilities, and whether or not they use the latest diagnostic equipment.

In other professions, health benefits, vacation time, sick days, profit sharing such as a 401(k), use of a company car, commission or salary, daycare facilities, flex time, availability of tuition reimbursement, or use of cafeteria or gym are considerations. Pick what is most beneficial to you personally. For some people, the availability of a comprehensive medical, dental, and vision plan or tuition reimbursement (for children) is more important than salary. Also consider that you may be able to receive a higher rate of pay (dollar-per-hour or cost-per-job rate) working on a freelance, contractual, or per diem basis because under such conditions the employer does not have to pay benefits.

JOB SEARCH FOLLOW-UP

It's critical that you follow up with prospective employers after applying for a position. E-mails are accidentally trashed, and resumes can be lost in cyberspace. Give the employer at least two weeks, and then if you have not heard back from the company, follow up with a phone call or e-mail asking if the company received your application and reiterate your interest in the position. Do not worry; you are not going to annoy potential employers with this approach. If anything, they will appreciate your interest, and the information you receive will determine when to contact them again or if you should cross them off your list and look elsewhere.

Sample Follow-Up Call

My name is Julie Moore. About three weeks ago I interviewed for the account manager position at your company. Can you tell me what the status of that position is? (Or, *Has the position been filled yet?*) *Thank you for the information.*

Sample Acceptance Letter

Dear Mr. Jones,

Thank you for offering me the position of Account Manager at ABC Media. I am delighted to accept your offer at a starting salary of $45,000 plus benefits and commission.

As we discussed, I will plan to begin my new position on August 1 and will then attend the four-day orientation and training program at your corporate headquarters in Reno.

Again, thank you for the opportunity to become a member of your team. I look forward to a successful career with your organization.

Sincerely,
Catherine Moore

Sample Letter Declining the Offer

Dear Mr. Jones,

Thank you for your offering me the Account Manager position at ABC Media. I enjoyed meeting with you and your staff and having the opportunity to learn about your operations. Your company is quite impressive, and you have a talented team of professionals in the sales and marketing department.

However, after careful consideration, I have decided to accept a position with another company that I believe will be a better fit. I am confident that whoever you hire will be fortunate to become a part of your team.

Thank you for your time and consideration, and I wish your company much success.

Sincerely,
Catherine Moore

Chapter 22

HOW TO FIND A JOB IN A TIGHT ECONOMY

Success is achieved and maintained by those who try and keep on trying with a positive mental attitude.

Napoleon Hill and W. Clement Stone

Ten years ago, it was a common joke that job candidates merely had to be breathing to be eligible for a job. It was a *hot* job market in 1999. The dot.com bubble was in full bloom, and instant stock-option millionaires were everywhere. It was not uncommon to find CEOs in their twenties, especially in start-up companies. It was a dream world for job seekers because employers were practically begging for candidates.

We have recently experienced one of the most competitive job markets since the Great Depression. That means you, the job seeker, must be very competitive in every aspect of your job search. In a tight job market, there are many more applicants than there are openings. It's an employer's job market. You must display your qualifications and demonstrate how you can be an asset to an employer.

While many employers' hiring projections have been flat, there are some industries that are hiring. Government employers are predicting a hiring *increase* of nearly 20 percent. The Civil Service is often an overlooked source of employment because of the cumbersome nature of the application process. However, the lengthy process may be worth the wait in light of the job stability and benefit packages Civil Service jobs offer. Because of a large number of pending retirements, there will be opportunities in the state and federal sector ranging from computer information technology and health care to juvenile justice, security, and engineering technology.

Traditionally, when the job market goes south, many people choose to return to school to pick up additional certifications, degrees, and anything else that will increase their marketability. Others take the opportunity, whether by choice or not, to change careers.

Here are some tips to increase your chances of finding a job in a tight economy:

- Start now. Do not wait until you quit your job, graduate from school, or your unemployment runs out. In a tight job market, it may take longer than anticipated to find a position. Start applying for advertised job openings, making contacts, attending job fairs, and inquiring about future openings as early as possible.

- Stress your skills and results on resumes and during interviews. Highlight the accomplishments you have accrued over your work history. If you returned to school to make a career change, highlight experience gained during clinicals, practica, student teaching, internships, research projects, or other related activities. Use a "Summary" of your past accomplishments and expertise, rather than an "Objective" on your resume. Bring a portfolio to the interview to illustrate your skills by providing sample lesson plans, journalism articles, art projects, engineering designs, research papers, marketing or sales promotions, business proposals, honors or awards received, or employee evaluations.

- Identify the types of jobs you are interested in and the employers you want to target by looking in the phone book, at company Web sites, and in business and industry directories or materials provided by chambers of commerce and professional organizations.

- Use multiple sources and a variety of methods to search for openings. Use online sources like Careerbuilder.com, Monster.com, dice.com (IT); the newspaper classifieds; Web sites of professional organizations; classified sections in trade or professional journals. Watch for help wanted signs posted next to businesses; ask friends, neighbors, or colleagues to help you locate openings. Attend all job fairs in your area, and register with your local One Stop Career Center, your local college career services, or a staffing or employment agency. Take advantage of all those contacts you made over the years and those you have acquired through LinkedIn or Facebook. Talk to former business contacts, clients, coworkers, neighbors, professors, alumni, and working professionals in the field to help you locate possible job openings.

- Actively search for jobs. Do not simply wait for job openings to appear in the newspaper. Approach companies you may be interested in working for and inquire about possible openings. Visit the employment section on their Web sites, and then call or e-mail their Human Resources Office and inquire about current or future openings. Send or give them a copy of your resume if they express an interest. A simple two-line e-mail inquiry can sometimes yield useful information.

- Be organized. Create a log and write down who you contacted. Include the date, the name of the company, the result of your contact, and the follow-up action needed or taken. Continue to follow up with each employer every two to four weeks as appropriate.

- Conduct your job search in a formal, professional manner. Dress, act, and communicate like a professional. Avoid using e-mail emoticons, casual text-messaging lingo, or wearing an outfit to an interview that is better suited for an evening with friends. That goes double for voicemail messages, e-mail addresses, and your Facebook profile.

- Widen your geographic distance when applying for jobs. If you are having difficulty finding a position, consider looking outside your normal geographic area and apply for positions you would otherwise consider too far away. Consider alternative transportation methods to defray the cost of gas.
- Be flexible and strategic. If you are unable to find a full-time position, take a part-time, temporary, consultant or per diem position and do not turn any opportunity down. Then, use that position to build your skills and experience while continuing to look for a better opportunity. Remember, in a tough economy, having *a* job is better than having no job at all.
- Consider registering with a temporary help service agency such as Manpower, One Source, or Kelly Services (check your local yellow pages under "Employment Services"), or register with a permanent staffing agency. Contact career-specific recruiters (many advertise on the Internet). Sometimes, temporary assignments lead to permanent positions. In any event, temporary assignments will bring in some extra cash in the meantime and help you gain more skills, experience, and references to put on your resume.

In a tight economy, job seekers need to look early and often, be creative, and utilize many different sources for job leads. Utilize your professional and social networks. You have to keep things in perspective when you are turned down for jobs that you may not have even entertained a year ago. Adjust to the marketplace. Well-qualified, well-educated applicants are plentiful these days. You need to be flexible and keep a positive attitude.

The main obstacle to overcome in a down economy is competing against the sheer number of applicants applying for each job. A company may get 100–200 applications and resumes, which they will sift through and then phone interview 30 and screen out another 15–20 candidates to bring the pool down to a manageable number of interviews. That's why online applications are so widely accepted and the use of applicant tracking software is so popular today. In a down economy, employers do not have to recruit—in fact, they are often deluged by an overwhelming number of applications even before the position is formally advertised. Nursing recruiters have told me that applicants should apply immediately rather than waiting. If a job opening comes out in the Sunday paper, by Tuesday the recruitment is already internally shut down because the recruiters have already received more applicants than they can deal with.

Looking for work is your job right now. Find leads and do lots of follow up. It pays to be persistent, especially in a tight market. At the same time, it does not pay to stress yourself out over trying to find a job. Search for a job for four hours a day at most. Then go have some fun and enjoy the rest of the day with your children, your family, or friends. Take care of your physical, emotional, and spiritual needs so you have the energy you need to look for work. You'll make a better impression in an interview if you are relaxed and positive. And above all else, be open to any opportunities that come your way.

Chapter 23

THE NEXT PHASE
OF YOUR LIFE

The future belongs to those who believe in their dreams.

Eleanor Roosevelt

DO NOT BURN BRIDGES

Changing careers does not mean you have to burn bridges at your former job. There are ways to part amicably with your company. In fact, you should try to part on good terms because you never know when you will meet up again in the future.

As soon as you have received a firm offer, in writing, from your new employer, notify your current employer. It is professionally courteous to give at least two weeks' notice, although it is not uncommon for individuals in key administrative or executive positions to give up to one month of advanced notice. You want to leave as you came in—as a professional. Offer to train your replacement, and thank everyone who helped you along the way. Unless you have a legitimate reason for doing so or are directly asked to express your opinions about your workplace, there is probably no benefit to be gained by badmouthing your boss, your coworkers, or the company. By choosing your words carefully, you can frame criticisms into helpful suggestions.

Meet with your human resources department to complete any required paperwork. Make sure you understand the company's policy about unused vacation or sick days and when your insurance benefits will be officially terminated. You may want to take advantage of your current medical insurance by scheduling doctor and dental visits and checkups before you leave.

BEGINNING YOUR NEW CAREER

Beginning a new job is difficult for anyone, whether it's the first job or the last job. Everything is new—from the phone system to the people you work with. Even figuring out where to park and what to do for lunch can be major stumbling blocks during those first few days on the job. Hopefully, someone will be assigned to help orient you to your new surroundings. Accept the fact that it will take some time to adjust to your new career, so be patient with yourself. Get to know the people that you are working with and the unspoken rules of the place by paying attention to what is going on around you. Use those transferable skills you developed in previous jobs to smooth the transition. Even though you may not know the specifics of your job yet, you still know how to take a phone call, call a meeting, or interview a potential client.

Here are some tips to help make the transition easier:

1. Make the announcements to the appropriate people and organizations about your change. Let any recruiters you were working with know about your new position so they do not make any further efforts on your behalf. Your network should also hear about the good news. Those who had a hand or who simply offered support will want to know that their efforts paid off. Remember, your network grows with each job, and it stays with you long beyond that job.
2. Write things down to help you remember all the information you are going to be exposed to during the first few days on the job. Take notes during your orientation, and make a cheat-sheet of the names of the people you meet, map the locations of places like the cafeteria and the office supply room, and jot down such common procedures as how to log onto your computer and how to process a travel expense form.
3. Give yourself time to adjust. Allow yourself the necessary time to become familiar with the job and its requirements. Take the initiative to become oriented to your new atmosphere, and learn as much as you can.
4. Try to let go of any bitterness, anger, insecurities, negative attitudes, or beliefs you may harbor from the place you left (i.e., being fired or laid off). This is your chance for a fresh start, so begin on an optimistic note.
5. Make friends. Go to lunch with your coworkers. Getting to know people in your office and those in related departments will help eliminate feelings of isolation and help you adjust.
6. Create some personal space for yourself at the office. Whether you have your own office, a cubicle, or just a desk, try to make your space your own. Put in some personal effects such as photos or decorations. Doing this will help you to feel more at home in the new work environment.
7. Pick a mentor. Try to find someone who has been on the job for a while who will answer your questions and show you the ropes.
8. Make a good impression. Just as in the interview, your bosses and coworkers are formulating a favorable or unfavorable impression of you during the first few days of your new job. Besides passing the mandatory probationary period, the first six months may make or break your professional career and any possibilities for advancement. Presenting yourself as a professional, displaying a willing and collegial attitude, and being careful and considerate in your duties will go a long way to creating a favorable reputation with your boss and coworkers.
9. Be professional and friendly to everyone until you understand the office politics and can formulate your own opinions about the people you work with. You do not want to damage your reputation in the early days

of your new career by saying the wrong thing to the wrong person. Try to avoid the gossips or wet blankets who may be a little too eager to recruit a newcomer to their side.

10. Observe and listen before offering opinions. Avoid expressing criticism or making suggestions until you learn all the facts, hear everyone's side of the story, and understand the big picture.

11. Program yourself for success. After you have finished reading policy manuals and attending new staff orientation meetings, what are your first projects? How can you make an early contribution? During the honeymoon period you have the opportunity to establish and position yourself for long-term success. Think through your project plans and establish goals and metrics for yourself, so you will know how you are doing. Consider the impact of your projects on the organization's vision and mission. And most important, pace yourself and do not try to do it all in an effort to make an early mark.

For those of you who went back to school to train for a new career, getting a job will be a welcome relief to cramming for exams. After months or years of being a student, you are probably more than ready to get out there and begin your new career.

Some of you may be starting your own business, which carries its own share of initial concerns. In an attempt to establish your business to the point where it will generate customers and supply a steady stream of income, you may find you are working longer hours than you anticipated. Maintaining a healthy balance between work and personal responsibilities will be critical during this phase.

REDEFINING RETIREMENT

When you do finally decide to retire from full-time employment, it makes sense to retire *to* something, not *from* something. This implies that you will need to make some kind of transition plan. After spending the better part of your adult life identifying with what you do, rather than who you are, it's illogical to expect yourself to immediately stop doing and being what you have been for the last 20 or 30 years without some kind of ill effect. Many people simply fall apart from a simple lack of structure after retirement. Each of us has a greater tolerance for doing nothing, but after two months of doing nothing, even the least industrious of us will begin to get a bit antsy. Boredom, inertia, loss of purpose, and loss of social interaction can lead to illness, divorce, chemical addiction, and depression.

Dr. Ken Dychtwald, author of *Age Power*,[1] describes retirement as a time of confusion and frustration for many workers, especially those whose identity is tied directly to their jobs. But it is also a time of growth and reinvention.

People who suddenly retire with no post-retirement plan seem to have a difficult time adjusting to the lack of structure, lack of social contact, and lack of doing something with their day. Those who continue to stay actively involved in something during their retirement through volunteer or paid work, social activities, a hobby, or learning something new, fared much better. I believe that those who are successful in retirement already have an arsenal of hobbies or activities at their disposal, and retirement is just a process of transferring one type of activity to another. Think of retirement as the time for realizing those things you always wanted to do but never had the time or opportunity, to do. That may mean enrolling in a creative writing class, learning to tie your own fly-fishing flies, or touring Europe. Retirement can be your time to kick back and enjoy a well-deserved rest, do all those things you never had the time to do before, or continue to pursue your hobbies or passions for as long as you are willing and able. However you decide to spend the third or fourth stage of your life, enjoy the journey!

Appendix: Resume Examples for Career Changers

Resume for a Marketing Manager Position

Kendra Jones

Professional Accomplishments

Management: Theatre at the Grove

- Developed nonprofit performing arts theater
- Oversaw operations of the theater and worked with production company
- Established committee and volunteer base

Sales: Five-Million-Dollar/Year Real Estate Business

- Achieved 20 years of million-dollar sales
- Obtained broker's license and managed office
- Maintained client database
- Created multilevel marketing plans

Public Service Director: WHAMS Radio Station

- Oversaw contests at Top 40 radio station
- Wrote, recorded, and scheduled Public Service Announcements (PSAs)
- Interviewed speakers and produced PSA spots

National Sales Manager: Brighton Industries, Inc.

- Oversaw 20 national sales representatives
- Traveled to reps' territories and resolved client issues
- Created National Trade Show booths and created show samples

Employment History

1989–2001	Real Estate Salesperson	Century 21 Real Estate, New Town, PA
1985–1989	National Sales Manager	Brighton Industries, New Town, PA
1982–1985	Public Service Director	WHAMS Radio Station, Wilkes-Barre, PA

Education

- Completed three years' undergraduate studies at American University and the University of New Haven

Community Involvement

- Currently Manage Lake Jean's Summer Theatre
- Served on Lake Jean's Borough Council
- Junior Warden of St. Paul's Church

References Available by Request

12 Main Street, New Town, PA 18721   517.123.4567   KJones@aol.com

RESUME TAILORED FOR A CUSTOMER SERVICE MANAGEMENT POSITION

Kendra Jones
12 Main Street, New Town, PA 18721
517.123.4567H 517.123.6678C
KJones@aol.com

Employment Skills

- Thrived in a fast-paced atmosphere
- Maintained excellent customer relations and developed customer rapport
- Diplomatically resolved customer complaints on an as-needed basis
- Motivated and supervised 20+ employees on a daily basis
- Successfully completed projects and made decisions with no supervision
- Consistently met quotas
- Proficiently employed Microsoft Office applications

Employment History

- *Associate Broker, Lee Smith Real Estate, 2001–Present*
- *Sales Associate, Century 21 Real Estate, 1989–2001*
- *Sales Manager, Brighton Industries, 1985–1989*
- *Public Service Director, WHAMS Radio Station, 1982–1985*
- *Director, Senior Craftsmen of Wyoming Valley, 1970s*

Education

- Completed three years' undergraduate studies at American University and the University of New Haven

Community Experience

- Currently Manage Lake Jean's Summer Theatre
- Served on Lake Jean's Borough Council
- Junior Warden of St. Paul's Church

References
Excellent references available by request

RESUMES BEFORE AND AFTER

Before: Traditional Format

David J. Jones
15 Apple Drive
Mountain Top, PA 18707
(570) 123-4567
Jonesdj@yahoo.com

EDUCATION	A.A.S., Cyber Security Management, May 2009
	Luzerne County Community College, Nanticoke, PA

MAJOR COURSEWORK

Systems Networking	Electrical Theory
Linux Operating Systems	Computer Forensics
PC Security and Network Security	
Windows XP and Vista Operating Systems	
Microcomputer Architecture and Multimedia Systems	

EXPERIENCE

2007–2009

Army National Guard, Pennsylvania

Signal System Support Specialist

- Installed, operated, and maintained designated radio and data distribution systems.
- Provided communication support.

2005–2006

U.S. Marine Corps, International

Embassy Security Guard

- Received Top Secret Security Clearance, SSBI, April 2005.
- Provided security for American embassies overseas.
- Protected American citizens and classified material.
- Provided security for the Secretary of State.

2001–2003

U.S. Marine Corps, Domestic, International

Supply and Logistics

- Supplied parts to deploying units.
- Worked in Shipping and Receiving.
- Tracked inventory.

After: Plain Text Format

David J. Jones
15 Apple Drive
Mountain Top, PA 18707
(570) 123-4567
Jonesdj@yahoo.com

EDUCATION
A.A.S., Cyber Security Management, May 2009
Luzerne County Community College, Nanticoke, PA

MAJOR COURSEWORK
Systems Networking, Electrical Theory
Linux Operating Systems, Computer Forensics
PC Security and Network Security
Windows XP and Vista Operating Systems
Microcomputer Architecture and Multimedia Systems

EXPERIENCE
Army National Guard, Pennsylvania
Signal System Support Specialist, 2007−2009
  * Installed, operated, and maintained designated radio and data distribution
    systems.
  * Provided communication support.

U.S. Marine Corps, International
Embassy Security Guard, 2005−2006
  * Received Top Secret Security Clearance, SSBI, April 2005.
  * Provided security for American embassies overseas.
  * Protected American citizens and classified material.
  * Provided security for the Secretary of State.
U.S. Marine Corps, Domestic, International
Supply and Logistics, 2001−2003
  * Supplied parts to deploying units.
  * Worked in Shipping and Receiving.
  * Tracked inventory.

SAMPLE COVER LETTER FOR TRADITIONAL MAIL

Your Name
Your Address
City, State Zip Code
Your Phone Number

Date of Letter

Employer's Name
Employer's Title
Name of Company
Company Address

Salutation: Use Title and Last Name (e.g., Dear Dr. Smith or Dear Ms. Jones); do not use a first name unless you know the individual well; if you do not have a name, use the title (e.g., Dear Employment Manager).

Opening Paragraph: State why you are writing, identify the name of the position or the type of work for which you are applying, and mention how you heard of the opening or organization.

Middle Paragraph(s): Here, you want to summarize your major strengths as they relate to the position you are seeking. Highlight one or two accomplishments that illustrate your proficiency and effectiveness. The idea is to create interest and show how your skills and qualifications can be of value to the organization. Do not reiterate everything that's in your resume; instead, refer the reader to your enclosed resume for more details on your qualifications and experience.

Closing Paragraph: Restate your strong interest in the position and your desire for an interview. State that you look forward to hearing from the reader soon, and provide your contact information. Finally, express your appreciation for the reader's time and consideration.

Sincerely,
(Write your full name in blue or black ink here.)
(Type your full name here.)
Enclosure

Sample E-Mail Cover Letter

To: scott.jones@ValleyView.com
Subject: Respiratory Therapy position

Dear Dr. Jones:

I recently completed an Associate of Science degree in Respiratory Therapy from Tripp Community College and wish to be considered for the full-time Respiratory Therapy position at ValleyView Memorial Hospital. I possess excellent verbal and written communication skills, work well with clients of all ages, and can maintain a calm presence during an emergency.

I have attached my resume for your review. I hope to discuss this position at your earliest convenience.

Thank You,
Your Name

(Place resume attachment here.)

NOTES

INTRODUCTION

1. T. Zeiss, *Build Your Own Career Ladder: Four Secrets to Making Your Career Dreams Come True* (Nashville, TN: Thomas Nelson, 2006).

CHAPTER 1

1. C. Strenger and A. Ruttenberg, "The Existential Necessity of Midlife Change," *Harvard Business Review* (February, 2008), http://hbr.harvardbusiness.org/2008/02/the-existential-necessity-of-midlife-change/ar/1 (accessed August 12, 2009).
2. W. Sadler, *Third Age: Six Principles for Personal Growth and Rejuvenation After Forty* (Cambridge, MA: Perseus Publishing, 2000).
3. L. S. Evans, "It's Time to Look at the 'Third Stage' of Life" *Northeast Pennsylvania Business Journal* 24, no. 6 (May 2009).
4. K. Columbia, "Addressing Generational Diversity," Goddard Space Flight Center, http://fpd.gsfc.nasa.gov/diversity/GenerationalDiversity.pdf (accessed August 11, 2009).
5. R. Zemke, C. Raines, and B. Filipczak, *Generations at Work* (New York: Performance Research Associates, 2000).
6. J. J. L'Allier and K. Kolosh, "Preparing for Baby Boomer Retirement," *RetirementCommunities.com* (June 2007), http://www.retirementcommunities.com/news_details.php?news=13 (accessed July 13, 2009).
7. M. Toossi, "Labor Force Projections to 2018: Older Workers Staying More Active," *Monthly Labor Review* 132, no. 11 (November 2009): 30–51.
8. G. Rainville, "AARP Bulletin Survey on Employment Status of the 45+ Population," *AARP* (May 2009), http://www.aarp.org/research/surveys/money/work/employment/articles/bulletin_jobs_09.html (accessed July 15, 2009).
9. M. Toossi, "Labor Force Projection to 2016: More Workers in Their Golden Years," *Monthly Labor Review* 130, no. 11 (November 2007): 33–52.
10. H. N. Fullerton and M. Toossi, "Labor Force Projections to 2010: Steady Growth and Changing Composition," *Monthly Labor Review* 124, no. 11 (November 2001): 21–38.
11. W. C. Borman, J. W. Hedge, and S. E. Lammlein, *The Aging Workforce* (Washington, DC: American Psychological Association, 2006).
12. N. Kareem, "The Second Act: Career Change vs. Retirement: Vitality, Lack of Funds Cited," *San Fernando Valley Business Journal* (October 1, 2007), http://findarticles.com/p/articles/mi_hb274/is_20_12/ai_n29408805/?tag=content;col1 (accessed June 15, 2009).

13. A. S. W. Roper, "Baby Boomers Envision Retirement II, Key Findings: Survey of Baby Boomers' Expectations for Retirement," *AARP Bulletin*, no. 24 (May 2004), http://assets.aarp.org/rgcenter/econ/boomers_envision_1.pdf (accessed May 11, 2009).

14. S. Groeneman and E. Pope, "Staying Ahead of the Curve, 2007: The AARP Work and Career Study" (Washington, DC: AARP Knowledge Management, 2008), http://assets.aarp.org/rgcenter/econ/work_career_08.pdf (accessed May 11, 2009).

15. Toossi, "Labor Force Projection to 2018."

16. MetLife Mature Market Institute, "Living Longer, Working Longer: The Changing Landscape of the Aging Workforce—a MetLife Study" (New York: MetLife Mature Market Institute, April 2006), http://www.metlife.com/assets/cao/mmi/publications/studies/mmi-studies-living-longer.pdf (accessed October 1, 2009).

17. MetLife, "Study of Employee Benefits Trends: Finding from the National Survey of Employers and Employees" (New York: Metropolitan Life Insurance Company, 2007), http://www.whymetlife.com/trends (accessed June 20, 2009).

18. Borman, Hedge, and Lammlein, *The Aging Workforce.*

19. M. Patrick-Vaughn, "A New Wave of (Older) Workers: Retiring Baby Boomers Could Create a New Workforce," *Vancouver Business Journal Online* (September 5, 2008), http://www.vbjusa.com/stories/2008-09-05/a_new_wave_of_older_workers.html (accessed July 14, 2009).

20. W. J. Waitrowski, "Changing Retirement Age: Ups and Downs," *Monthly Labor Review* 124 (2001): 3–12.

21. History.com, "Life Span" (2006), *History.com*, http://www.history.com/encyclopedia.do?articleId=214788 (accessed September 23, 2009).

22. Ibid.

23. Population Division of the Department of Economic and Social Affairs of the United Nations Secretariat, "World Population Prospects: The 2008 Revision," http://esa.un.org/unpp/ (accessed July 1, 2009).

24. M. Hitti, "Life Expectancy Hovers Just Below 78 Years," *WebMD* (February 28, 2005), http://www.webmd.com/news/20050228/us-life-expectancy-best-ever-says-cdc (accessed September 30, 2009).

25. T. S. Salthouse, "Effects of Age and Skill on Typing," *Journal of Experimental Psychology* 13 (1984): 345–71.

26. Borman, Hedge, and Lammlein, *The Aging Workforce.*

27. M. Freedman, *Encore: Finding Work That Matters in the Second Half of Life* (New York: Public Affairs, 2008).

28. Diagnosis Dictionary, "Midlife," *Psychology Today*, http://www.psychologytoday.com/conditions/mid-life (accessed July 15, 2009).

29. R. W. Johnson, J. Kawachi, and E. K. Lewis, "Older Workers on the Move: Recareering in Later Life," *AARP.org* (May 2009), http://www.aarp.org/research/work/employment/2009_08_recareering.html (accessed July 15, 2009).

30. G. D. Cohen, *The Mature Mind: The Positive Power of the Aging Brain* (New York: Basic Books, 2005).

Chapter 2

1. A. Wrzesniewski, C. McCauley, P. Rozin, and B. Schwartz, "Jobs, Careers, and Callings: People's Relations to Their Work," *Journal of Research in Personality* 31, no. 1 (1997): 21–33.

2. G. D. Cohen, *The Mature Mind: The Positive Power of the Aging Brain* (New York: Basic Books, 2005).

3. H. Zelon, "Live & Learn," *AARP* (Summer 2007), http://www.aarp.org/aarp/live_ and_learn/Transitions/articles/If_Not_Now_When_.html (accessed June 4, 2009).

4. CareerBuilder, "Half of Workers Who Were Laid Off in the Last Three Months Found Jobs," *CareerBuilder.com*, http://www.careerbuilder.com/share/aboutus/pressre leasesdetail.aspx?id=pr491&sd=4/8/2009&ed=04/08/2009 (accessed September 15, 2009).

CHAPTER 3

1. S. Groeneman, "Staying Ahead of the Curve 2007: The AARP Work and Career Study" (Washington, DC: AARP Knowledge Management, 2008).

CHAPTER 5

1. J. Lahey, "Age, Women and Hiring: An Experimental Study" (Boston: Center for Retirement Research at Boston College, 2006).

2. R. Skladany, "Age Bias in the American Workplace: A 'Fact of Life' Enters Its Own Phased Retirement" (Wellesley, MA: RetirementJobs.com, 2007), http://www.retire-mentjobs.com/research/bias_paper.pdf (accessed July 14, 2009).

3. Wisconsin Department of Workforce Development, "Myths About Older Workers" (June 22, 2001), www.dwd.state.wi.us/olderworker/pdf/myths_about_Older_workers. pdf (accessed May 15, 2009).

4. B. Skladany, "Myths About Older Workers: The Truth Will Set You Free," *AARP*, http://www.aarp.org/money/work/articles/myths_about_older_workers.html (accessed May 15, 2009).

5. National Association of Colleges and Employers, "Job Outlook, 2009" (Bethlehem, PA: National Association of Colleges and Employers 2008).

6. Wisconsin Department of Workforce Development, "Myths About Older Workers" (June 22, 2001), http://www.dwd.state.wi.us/olderworker/pdf/myths_about_Older_ workers.pdf (accessed May 15, 2009).

CHAPTER 6

1. S. Steiner, "Americans Feel Secure About Jobs," *Bankrate.com*, http://www.bankrate. com/finance/financial-literacy/older-workers-hit-harder-by-economy-1.aspx (accessed June 23, 2009).

2. L. Macko and K. Rubin, *Midlife Crisis at 30: How the Stakes Have Changed for a New Generation—and What to Do About It* (New York: Rodale, 2004).

3. E. A. Colozzi, "Career Across Your Lifespan," *Career Developments* 25, no. 3 (2009): 5–9.

4. A. E. M. van Vianen, I. E. De Pater, and P. T. Y. Preenen, "Adaptable Careers: Maximiz-ing Less and Exploring More," *Career Development Quarterly* 57, no. 4 (2009): 298–309.

5. For more reading, see J. D. Krumboltz, K. E. Mitchell, and A. S. Levin, "Planned Hap-penstance: Constructing Unexpected Career Opportunities," *Journal of Counseling & Development*, 77, no. 2 (1999): 115–24.

6. C. Strenger and A. Ruttenberg, "The Existential Necessity of Midlife Change," *Harvard Business Review* (February 2008), http://hbr.harvardbusiness.org/2008/02/the-existential-necessity-of-midlife-change/ar/1 (accessed August 12, 2009).

7. van Vianen, De Pater, and Preenen, "Adaptable Careers."

CHAPTER 7

1. Bureau of Labor Statistics, "Employment Projections: 2008-2018," news release (December 10, 2009), http://www.bls.gov/news.release/ pdf/ecopro.pdf (accessed December 11, 2009).
2. Ibid.
3. Ibid.
4. M. C. Moskowitz, "Academic Health Center CEOs Say Faculty Shortages Major Problem" (Washington, DC: Association of Academic Health Centers, 2007), http://www.aahcdc.org/policy/reddot/AAHC_Faculty_Shortages.pdf (accessed September 9, 2009).
5. Bureau of Labor Statistics, "Employment Projections: 2008-2018."
6. M. Freedman, *Encore: Finding Work That Matters in the Second Half of Life* (New York: Public Affairs, 2008).
7. MetLife Foundation / Civic Ventures, "New Face of Work Survey" (San Francisco: Civic Ventures, 2005), http://www.civicventures.org/publications/surveys/new-face-of-work.cfm (accessed June 17, 2009).
8. R. Elgie, "Politics, Economics, and Nursing Shortages: A Look at U.S. Policies," *Medscape*, http://www.medscape.com/viewarticle/565608_5 (accessed May 11, 2009).
9. R. Donley and M. J. Flaherty, "Revisiting the American Nurses Association's First Position on Education for Nurses: A Comparative Analysis of the First and Second Position Statements on the Education of Nurses," *Online Journal of Issues in Nursing* 7, no. 2 (2002), http://nursingworld.org/MainMenuCategories/ANAMarketplace/ANAPeriodicals/OJIN/TableofContents/vol132008/No2May08/ArticlePreviousTopic/EntryIntoPracticeUpdate.aspx (accessed May 11, 2009).
10. American Association of Colleges of Nursing, "Nursing Shortage Fact Sheet," fact sheet (2009), http://www.aacn.nche.edu/Media/FactSheets/NursingShortage.htm (accessed May 11, 2009).
11. P. I. Buerhaus, V. Potter, D. O. Staiger, J. French, and D. I. Auerbach, *The Future of the Nursing Workforce in the United States: Data, Trends and Implications* (Boston: Jones and Bartlett, 2009).
12. The Information Company, "Choosing a Career That Offers Big Potential," *Careerism Newsletter* 40, no. 3 (2009): 10−11.

CHAPTER 8

1. States' Career Cluster Initiative, "16 Career Clusters," http://www.careerclusters.org/16clusters.cfm (accessed September 21, 2009).
2. Carnegie Mellon, "Pathways to a Teaching Career," http://www.psy.cmu.edu/~kidsweb/Pathways/Alternative/ALT.html (accessed October 1, 2009).
3. Internal Revenue Service, "Tax-Exempt Status for Your Organization," Department of the Treasury, Publication 557, cat. no. 46573C (June 2008), http://www.irs.gov/pub/irs-pdf/p557.pdf (accessed March 20, 2009).
4. National Center for Charitable Statistics, "National Taxonomy of Exempt Entities," http://nccs.urban.org/classification/NTEE.cfm (accessed March 20, 2009).
5. L. G. Otting, *Change Your Career: Transitioning to the Nonprofit Sector: Shifting Your Focus from the Bottom Line to a Better World* (New York: Kaplan Publishing, 2007).

Chapter 9

1. H. Ibarra, *Working Identity: Unconventional Strategies for Reinventing Your Career* (Boston: Harvard Business School Press, 2003).

Chapter 10

1. Bureau of Labor Statistics, "Employment Projections 2008-2018," news release (December 10, 2009), http://www.bls.gov/news.release/pdf/ecopro.pdf (accessed December 11, 2009).
2. Ibid.
3. Ibid.
4. Bureau of Labor Statistics, "Education and Income: More Learning Is Key to Higher Earnings," *Occupational Outlook Quarterly* 50, no. 3 (2006): 60.

Chapter 12

1. D. Connaughton, S. Hanton, and G. Jones, "What Is This Thing Called Mental Toughness? An Investigation of Elite Sport Performers," *Journal of Applied Sport Psychology* 14, no. 3 (2002): 205–18.
2. D. Yukelson, "What Is Mental Toughness and How to Develop It?" Penn State University, http://www.mascsa.psu.edu/dave/Mental-Toughness.pdf (accessed August 12, 2009).

Chapter 13

1. Bureau of Labor Statistics, "Unemployed Jobseekers by Age, Sex, Race, Hispanic or Latino Ethnicity, and Active Jobsearch Methods Used" (2008, Table 33), ftp://ftp.bls.gov/pub/special.requests/lf/aat33.txt (accessed June 22, 2009).
2. S. Steiner, "Americans Feel Secure About Jobs," *Bankrate.com* (June 5, 2009), http://www.bankrate.com/finance/financial-literacy/older-workers-hit-harder-by-economy-1.aspx (accessed June 23, 2009).

Chapter 14

1. For more information, see A. Doyle, *Internet Your Way to a New Job* (Cupertino, CA: Happy About, 2008).

Chapter 18

1. J. J. Cotter, "Job Search Tips for Older Workers," *SignonSanDiego.com* (2009), http://careers.signonsandiego.com/johncotter/jc-olderworkers-20.php (accessed June 23, 2009).

Chapter 19

1. National Association of Colleges and Employers, "Job Outlook, 2009" (Bethlehem, PA: National Association of Colleges and Employers, 2008).
2. J. C. Franklin, "An Overview of BLS Projections to 2016," *Monthly Labor Review* 130, no. 11 (2007): 3–11, http://www.bls.gov/opub/mlr/2007/11/art1full.pdf (accessed April 6, 2009).
3. National Association of Colleges and Employers, "Job Outlook, 2009."

CHAPTER 20

1. A. J. Wise and L. J. Millward, "The Experiences of Voluntary Career Change in 30-Somethings and Implications for Guidance," *Career Development International* 10, no. 5 (2005): 400−419.

CHAPTER 23

1. K. Dychtwald, *Age Power: How the 21st Century Will Be Ruled by the New Old* (New York: Penguin Group, 2000).

Index

AARP, 1; best employers, 5, 40; surveys, 2, 3, 7, 22, 35
Abilities, 45
Accomplishments, 29
Accounting careers, 53
Adult students, 85
Age discrimination, 35; avoiding on resume, 93; survey, 35
Age expectancy. *See* Life span
Age-friendly occupations, 53
Aging workforce, impact upon, 4
Agriculture careers, 59
Americorps, 75
Art careers, 60
Associate degree, 83, 88

Baby boomers, 1, 78; encore careers, 54; retiring, 4; second careers, 53; work ethic, 37
Bachelor's degree, 81, 83, 89; and jobs, 84
Balance. *See* Work and life balance
Bankrate survey, 41, 109
Best employers, workers over 50, 5
Blog, 117
Bureau of Labor Statistics, earnings, 88; employment projections, 51–52, 81–82; methods finding work, 182; women participation rate, 3; worker shortages, 4
Burning bridges, 163
Business careers, 53, 60–61
Business casual, 133–34

Calment, Jeanne, 5
Career, and abilities, 45; attitude towards, 21; beginning new, 163–65; control over, 18; decision-making styles, 45; descriptions, 59; doers vs. advisors, 56; and economy, 55; encore, 97; factors to consider, 51; good second choices, 52–53; green, 67; myths, 45; non-profit, 67–68; number of, 4; outsource-proof, 54–55; recession-proof, 55; relationship to major, 83–84; researching, 46, 68–69, 77; and self-concept, 46; turn hobby into, 57; worker shortages, 51
Career assessments. *See* Interest inventory
Career change, 4; decisions, 18; decreasing risk, 76; economic conditions, 7; factors to consider, 51; and fear of, 17; financial assistance, 86–87; financing, 75; good second choices, 52–53; into hobby, 57; involuntary, 16; job or occupation, 10; late in life, 7; in midlife, 6, 15; planning for, 71, 73, 77, 101; reasons for, 11; reframing experience, 124; researching, 46–47, 77; and salary, 152–53; transferable skills, 27–28, 149; if undecided,

59; unplanned, 77−79; wishing
for, 9
Career clusters, 59
Career development, 44
Career life, 44
Career plan, 15, 71, 80; in midlife, 6
Career summary, 94, 95
Career trends, 51−52; over life span, 4
CareerBuilder survey, 16
Careerism Report, 56
Civic Ventures, 54
Classifieds, 119; decoding ads, 120−22
Clerical careers, 53
Cohen, Gene, 7, 11
College, 10 major myths, 87−89; and
adult students, 85; delivery
options, 85; and employment,
83; paying for, 75, 86−87;
success in, 85
College major, 83−84;
entrepreneurship, 84; liberal arts,
84; and minors, 84; professional
degrees, 84
Communications careers, 61−62
Consulting, 94
Contact log, 110−11
Counseling careers, 64−65
Cover letter, 96, 99

Distance interviewing, 116
Dychtwald, Ken, 165

Education, and salary, 56; economic
effect, 55; lack of, 81−82; majors
to careers, 83−84; paying for,
66−67; service programs, 75; tax
breaks for, 75
Education careers, 95, 142; age friendly
occupation, 53; career transition
to, 52; sample occupations, 62;
transferable skills, 52
Elevator pitch. *See* Marketing pitch
Employers, soft-skills, 145−48
Encore career, 6, 54
EnCorps Teacher Initiative, 75

Engineering careers, 62−63
Entrepreneurship, 57; college degree, 84

Facebook, 114−15
Financial services careers, 5
Free Application for Federal Student Aid, 87
Freedman, Marc, 6, 54

Generation X, 1, 2
Government careers, 66
Green careers, 67

Health care careers, 52, 63−64; age-
friendly, 53; second career, 52−53
Home business, 58
Hope and Lifetime Learning Credit, 75
Hospitality careers, 53, 64

Ibarra, Herminia, 76
Ideal job, 22, 24
Information technology careers, 65
Instant messaging, 115
Interest inventory, 45
Internet, and employers, 117; for job
search, 113
Interview, after, 155−56; appearance,
133−34; asking about salary,
153; asking questions, 134−35;
attitude, 142; begins when, 129;
challenging questions, 140−42;
commonly asked questions,
138−39; deal with rejection,
104; follow-up letters, 145;
industry-specific questions, 140;
maintaining composure, 103;
nervousness, 139; practice, 138;
preparation for, 132−33; pre and
post checklists, 143−44;
psychological testing, 131−32;
recovering from bad, 139−40;
researching company, 132−33;
tell me about yourself, 25; types
of, 130−31; using portfolio, 128;
via distance, 116
Interview Stream, 116

Jaques, Elliott, 1
Job, applying for, 30; beginning new, 163–65; change, 10; ideal, 22, 24: leaving, 163; satisfying, 24; unhappiness, 9
Job description, 83, 123, 138; and portfolio, 126; in resume, 98
Job duties, 25, 59, accomplishments, 29; in ads, 119–23; in resume, 96, 98; work environment, 15
Job market, tight, 159–61
Job openings, choosing, 40
Job search, 107, 113; applying online, 114; contact log, 110–11; decoding ads, 119; finding openings, 108–09; follow-up, 156–58; and mental toughness, 101–102; networking, 109–10; reading descriptions, 138; taking control, 104; in a tight market, 159–61; using a portfolio, 125; using ads, 119; using social networking sites, 114–15; using the internet, 113; waiting, 102–03; Web sites, 111–13
Job search engines, 111, 113
Job shadowing, 47
Job skills. See Skills
Jung, Carl, 41

Keywords, 95, 98, 208; in online applications, 98

Laid off, 77–79
Legal careers, 65–66
Life span, 5, 45
LinkedIn, 114–15

Macko, Lia, 42
Marketing pitch, 29–30, 137
Math careers, 118
Mental toughness, 101–02
MetLife survey, 3, 54

Middle age. See Midlife
Midlife, 1; and balance, 42; and career change, 6, 15; meaning and purpose, 41; non-profit careers, 67–68; reevaluation, 7; and values, 11
Midlife crisis, 1, 6
Midlife Crisis at 30, 42
Myers-Briggs Type Indicator, 22, 45

National Association of Colleges and Employers, 37; employer survey, 145
Networking, 109–10
Nonprofit organizations, 67–68

Occupational research, 46, 68–69
Older workers: age friendly occupations, 53; benefits of, 37–38; best employers, 40; dispelling myths, 39; and job performance, 5; myths and stereotypes, 36–37; top qualities, 37–38
One Stop Career Center, 86
Online job boards, 113
Outsource-proof, 54–55
Own business. See Entrepreneurship

Paying for school, 86–87
Peace Corps, 75
People, Data, or Things, 48
Phased retirement, 5
Planned happenstance, 45
Portfolio, 125; design, 127–28; in interview, 128; items to include, 125; organizing, 126–27
Professional degree, 56

Quality of life, 5

Real estate careers, 53
Recession-proof, 55; with education, 81
References, 92, 161; in portfolio, 126; in resume, 96–97; in interview, 133, 143

Resume, 158; action verbs, 96; career change language, 99; career summary, 30–33, 94; common mistakes, 98; deemphasizing age, 92–93; email, 98, 114; length, 97; listing accomplishments, 29; listing job duties, 98; new vs. old rules, 95–97; references, 96–97; scannable, 98; skills, 30–33; soft skills, 95; targeting to ads, 120; video, 115–16

Retirement, by industry, 4; redefined, 6, 165–66; trends, 3; workers reaching, 36

Rubin, Kerry, 42

Salary, 123; and career change, 152–53; factors to consider, 151–52; negotiating, 153; request for history, 151; Web sites, 154

Sales careers, 52, age-friendly occupation, 53

Second career, 52–53

Scannable resume, 98

Science careers, 66

Self-Directed Search, 45

Shoulds, 47

Skills, 25–26; commonly used, 26; in resume, 30–33; industry specific, 149; soft, 95, 145–48; through education, 26; transferable, 27–28

Social networking sites, 114–15

Soft skills, 95, 145–48

Strong Interest Inventory, 45

30-second commercial. See Marketing pitch

Teach for America, 75

Teaching, second career, 52–53

Tell me about yourself, 25

Trade Act, 86

Transferable skills, 27–28, 149

Transportation careers, 53, 67

Troops to Teachers, 75

Twitter, 115

Unemployed: career change, 77–79; paying for school, 86

Values. See Work values

Video interviewing, 116

Video resumes, 115–16

VISTA, 75

Women, and career change, 7, in 30's, 42; in the labor force, 3; life span, 5; marketing themselves, 137; reasons for working, 3

Work, 4; attitude towards, 21; and boredom, 15; environment, 23–24; financial aspects, 13; and meaning, 10; no advancement, 13; and personality type, 15; personal meaning, 13; physical reactions, 14; reasons for, 41; and unhappiness, 9; values, 12, 22

Work and life balance, 5, 42, 44, 165

Work ethic, 37

Work experience, but no degree, 82; skills, 26

Work values, 12, 22

Workers, reaching retirement, 36; shortage, 4, 51

Workforce, graying of, 2

Wrzesniewski, Amy, 10

About the Author

Mary E. Ghilani, MS, NCC, is the Director of Career Services at Luzerne County Community College in Pennsylvania where she provides career assessment, counseling, and job search assistance to college students and community members. She is the author of *10 Strategies for Reentering the Workforce: Career Advice for Anyone Who Needs a Good (or Better) Job Now* (Praeger, 2009), *Web-Based Career Counseling,* and several career-related articles. Her areas of expertise are career assessment, job-search strategies, career change, and Internet resources. She is a member of the American Counseling Association, the National Career Development Association, and the National Association of Colleges and Employers.